out of the void
the primal scream story

brendan
yates

EMPIRE
Publications

EMPIRE PUBLICATIONS
1 Newton Street, Manchester M1 1HW
copyright Brendan Yates 2003

ISBN 1 901 746 36 4

Jacket design: Ashley Shaw
Edited by Ashley Shaw and Stuart Fish

Back Cover: (from top to bottom) Primal Scream c1986; the line-up in 1990; Bobby on stage 2002; 'Star' promotion 1997.

Printed in Great Britain by:
Ashford Colour Press, Gosport, Hampshire

contents

illustrations

picture credits

*All photographs from the author's personal
collection; Every effort has been made to
trace copyright holders and we apologise in
advance for any unintentional omission.
We would be pleased to insert the
appropriate acknowledgement in any
subsequent edition.*

acknowledgements

"To steal from one author is plagiarism, to steal from many is research..."

The author wishes to thank Ashley Shaw and Stuart Fish at *Empire Publications* and others for their help and encouragement with the writing of this book, including Adele Emm, Nadine Cossigny, Tony Fletcher, Christine Longinotti, Jeff Birgbauer and John Robb.

My credit to the following writers whose quotes and or reviews I've used: Steve Sutherland and Andrew Harrison in various, Stuart Bailie, James Brown, James Oldham, Stuart Maconie, Roger Morton, David Swift, Danny Kelly, April Long, Neil Taylor and Stephen Dalton in the *NME*, Miranda Sawyer, Tom Doyle, Mark Ellen, Kerry Potter, Giles Smith and Andrew Collins in *Q*, John Harris, Andrew Perry, Adam Higginbotham, Rupert Howe, Sylvia Patterson, David Cavanagh and Andrew Male in *Select*, The Stud Brothers, Tony Naylor, Michael Bonner and Martin James in *Melody Maker*, Tom Lanham and Michael Krugman in *Raygun*, Ann Scanlon in *Sounds*, Bruce

Dessau in *Jamming!*, Tim Tooher in *Mojo*, John Reed in *Record Collector*, Simon King in *Jockey Slut*, Lee Harpin in *The Face*, Andy Cowan in *Rage* and Johnny Cigarettes in *Loaded*.

from the author

It was always my intention to keep this book short and snappy in a dot-to-dot way and to be relatively complimentary. The reasons for this are because Primal Scream are just a band who've made some crazy records for the times and much of what they've been through and how they've presented themselves has almost been as admirable as it has been amazing.

It's a book that in places should be taken as seriously as one of Bobby Gillespie's interviews.

Amen,

Brendan Yates,

September 2003

PS: I'm not concerned with poring over lyrics with a magnifying glass, that's another book.

brixton academy: december '02

The minute you stepped from the tube at Brixton station you could hear the cry, "Any tickets needed? Primal Scream... any tickets, selling here..." Surrounding the venue seedy salesmen attempted to sell bootleg posters, T-shirts, badges and tickets to the thousands of people milling around the Academy, where Primal Scream were about to perform the second of two nights to promote their album *Evil Heat*.

It was a seriously sold out show; the tickets, officially priced at a hefty twenty five pounds, were changing hands at four times that amount to fans desperate to get in whatever the cost.

It was December and biting cold, yet several devotees were seemingly unaffected by the conditions; many wore long-sleeved shirts inscribed with everything from "PRML SCRM MTHR FCKR" to the celebrated sunshine artwork from their third album that had identified the band for more than a decade. Everyone looked excited about seeing them at a venue they'd played many times over the years, but that night things seemed just a little different from before.

The album had been released back in August and

save for a few showpiece performances for TV and the odd appearance at outdoor festivals in the summer, this was the first time in their history that Primal Scream had failed to tour upon an album's release, the sales of which were consequently sluggish compared to previous efforts. Meanwhile press interest in the band (the members of which were now all aged around forty) had noticeably waned in favour of that for younger, supposedly more exciting acts.

Yet almost five thousand people filled the Brixton Academy hoping that Primal Scream could deliver as usual. Far from being novices when it comes to playing shows like this; Bobby Gillespie and company have criss-crossed Britain many times over the years, presenting brave versions of rock 'n' roll to audiences expecting everything from a simple fun night out to intense, energized and brutal lessons in world politics. As a result, and despite the lack of hype and press interest in the band, the public knew it was virtually guaranteed that they would put on a good show - word of mouth seemed to be the only advertisement required for this particular night.

Once inside, as in all venues like this, people crowded the cloakrooms and official merchandise stalls where T-shirts were going for roughly twice the price of those outside. Bouncers hurried people past the doors, young girls with pigtails collected for charity and folks were heard complaining about the price of a vodka and coke. In the auditorium the first band played to polite applause, though their sound was largely lost in the cavernous room that soon filled to three quarters full for the arrival of Black Rebel Motorcycle Club.

Unlike their headliners, BRMC had been receiving rave notices in recent months and some in the crowd had turned up solely to see them. Their leather outfits didn't do much to absorb light onto their silhouetted figures as they roamed the darkened stage, but they didn't disappoint, with an exciting set of up-tempo thrash pop numbers laced with fittingly lazy vocals. By the time they'd left the stage a crush had developed down the front.

The lights came back on as people filtered away to toilets and bars while many couples got far too engrossed in each other to notice the hardworking road crews rearranging the stage. When everyone was suitably refreshed, standing shoulder to shoulder down in the stalls or sat comfortably up on the balcony, the lights dimmed to a deep roar of excitement.

Primal Scream took to the stage at a quarter after midnight. First to appear was stick-thin singer Bobby

Gillespie, dressed in tight jeans and a baggy black gents' shirt which sailed behind him as he skipped lightly to his mic stand. Robert 'Throb' Young was next, grinning from ear to ear while strapping on his six string and quickly going through an array of camp poses as if all his work was already done.

Andrew Innes, smartly buttoned-up to the collar, was obviously far more concerned that his guitar was running okay. Then came bassman Mani in leather trousers and an equally tasteless tracksuit top yelling above the din, unaided by amplification, 'come on, let's 'ave it!'.

In the shadows stage left settled the noisy guitar guy Kevin Shields, who looked like he hadn't washed his hair in a millennium. Martin Duffy, the most genuine musician of the lot, positioned himself behind his keyboards and held his breath. Drummer Darrin Mooney's snare cracked and they were off into 'Accelerator', the loudest song they'd ever recorded.

Down at the front it was impossible to see anything but blinding blue strobe lights and occasional flashes of the band throwing themselves into it as if their very lives depended on it. People were pushing and shoving, elbows were flying around and oxygen was in ever shorter supply. The sound of them attacking their instruments blasted distortedly onto a tense crowd about to take out their frustrations in a gloriously communal and celebratory way.

Fringe hung permanently over his eyes, Gillespie swung his mic stand into the air in time to the line "come on, hit the accelerator, hit the accelerator," like a hybrid of Johnny Rotten and Iggy Pop.

For years Gillespie has been laughed at by the British music press as perhaps the least charismatic frontman who ever had the cheek to call himself a rock star. Yet he has always believed in himself and his band and, helped in no small way by the thousands of fans now at his feet imitating his famous spastic dancing, you would have to conclude that he'd finally developed as a successful rock 'n' roll performer. If you had a second to think that is...

Evil Heat's first single, the buzzing disco hymn 'Miss Lucifer' was next up. After just one song it was clear that only the brave or the foolish would want to stay down the front where things had already got far too physical for comfort. Up on stage Primal Scream had it easy as their driving riff exploded with deafening yells of 'shake it baby, shake it baby', that was sung louder by the audience.

Through numbers like 'Rise', 'Shoot Speed/Kill Light' and 'Pills', things calmed down to an extent, but it wasn't until the recent single 'Autobahn 66' that things finally dropped down below a hundred miles per hour. On record the song is a beautiful, melancholic affair; live, it was enhanced almost enough to fit tidily with the astoundingly arresting introduction.

In mid-set arrived 'Rocks', a song that had given the band their first top ten hit more than eight years before. It never sounded distinctly like Primal Scream - as no one song can - and it came from a period in their history that's not remembered with great fondness. When it came out they were called 'dance traitors' by sections of the media, but seeing it performed that night made that particular accusation look rather laughable. The Stones-esque guitars rattled in and people were going wild. Gillespie was running all over the stage working the crowd, swinging his slender hips and flicking around his bouncy black hair. Even the usually unflappable Robert Young seemed to forget himself and get right into it.

Within the band were former members of The Jesus And Mary Chain, Felt, The Stone Roses and My Bloody Valentine; four of the most acclaimed, important and wonderful alternative acts Britain has produced in the past twenty years.

It was an array of talent particular to a band that continues to defy standard music convention. Primal Scream have been routinely courageous and innovative, factors which go to explain the ability of their music to survive a multitude of differing styles. Yet on this night almost every song was presented in the same vicious, fist-clenching way.

By the time the set had rattled through the sonic bass attack of 'Kowalski' and the pulverising disco of 'Swastika Eyes', it became clear that things were never going to slow down during the first set at all. Though equally known for their dreamy ballads and delightful mid-tempo dance experiments, Primal Scream were unmistakably sticking to their formidable catalogue of electro punk rockers like a band possessed.

'Skull X', one particular overload from *Evil Heat*, saw them right on top of their game. The lashing distortion of overworked guitars and smacking drums was hardly pierced by Gillespie's forlorn vocals that exploded into screaming rants of desperation.

After an hour or so they left to thunderous applause and regrouped backstage. The ovation continued, everyone clapping in unison, shouting requests for old favourites and stamping their feet. When they returned the stage was in darkness; Gillespie mumbled an introduction to 'Higher Than The Sun' and immediately people were transfixed.

For many the song remains their greatest ever, and live, again far from the dreamy space pop on record, it was a compelling, heavy blast of what could be described as punk blues, that spiralled into a cacophonous frenzy of percussion and keyboard effects.

Returning to the set after the best part of a decade's absence was 'Jailbird', a monster Zeppelin-esque riff that saw Young and Innes expertly playing off against each other while Gillespie and Mani clasped like Jagger and Wyman strutting across '....Satisfaction' or 'Jumpin' Jack Flash'. It was a cleansing and picturesque sight to see them up there; soaked in sweat, giving their all for the fans who'd waited for hours and forked out a small fortune for tickets.

"We've had a great time," announced Gillespie to universal applause, while Mani, after one of his successful attempts to hijack the microphone, just said a long thank you to everyone including his musical influences.

'Movin' On Up', towards the end of the set, had Innes clapping above his head - perhaps wishing himself to be Phil Collins - and everyone else just lavishly harmonising, punching the air on the beat clearly wanting the night to go on and on. The last song was the hands in the air 'Kick Out The Jams'. It was an old MC5 song but Primal Scream have played it so many times over the years that it is now virtually theirs by default. They had played for an hour and a half.

Primal Scream weren't perfect that night, far from it, but no one seemed to care. Gillespie was typically slurred with his vocals, they missed chords and pretty much all night had the needles glued in the red in a room where for those down the front each breath might have been their last. Many fans left for the exits a stone lighter in weight - tired, bruised and aching, but perhaps that was the point. As a certain member of the band often feels compelled to point out, they were not too old, nor were they past it.

They killed.

beginnings

Bobby Gillespie has always been fascinated by the cult of rock 'n' roll; from Elvis to The Sex Pistols, via The Beatles, The Stones and virtually every manner of funky glam rock, the Glasgow boy of the 60s grew up hearing all the hits of the day. By the time Bobby was fifteen he had decided that he'd done enough observing and wanted to get involved - it was the beginning of a long and turbulent road.

As with so many tales of great musical excess, turmoil and innovation, the story of Primal Scream has modest beginnings. No one in the band had the luxury of an easy upbringing in comfortable Britain. It was never like that. Yet the working class pride generated by Glasgow's hugely successful shipyards has had a long lasting impact on many of the key people involved in the story.

Musically, the city had contributed relatively little to Britain's hip roster of artists but that didn't mean there hadn't been the unrest that always motivates young people to seek their own identity through music. Thus, with the decline of the shipbuilding industry, the former 'Second City of Empire' had become an untidy place, left with a depressed economy and high levels of unemployment. It was the home of Robert Gillespie, a proud trade union activist and anti-racist campaigner. Named after him, his son Bobby was born on 22 June 1962.

During an interview with the *New Musical Express*, Bobby junior explained: "My earliest memory is a dream I had when I was little, living in a tenement in Glasgow. I walked up the side of the building, and over the roof, then down the other side of the building. So my first memory is also the first dream I can ever remember having, which is a bit strange." Later, when asked what characteristics he'd inherited from his parents, he simply replied: "Socialism and a sense of humour."

When Bobby was ten the family were living in a featureless suburb north of the town called Springburn. Around this time he recalls being puzzled by the sight of drunken men staggering out of pubs and stumbling home. As a boy Bobby couldn't comprehend exactly why they had to damage themselves like this. His father was a drinker and soon afterwards his younger brother Graham got in trouble, yet Bobby was a well-behaved adolescent, and much as he remains to this day hardly interested in cigarettes or alcohol. Bobby wasn't a wholly introverted young man, but he did keep well clear of serious trouble. In the early 70s the family moved to the suburb of Mount Florida, close to Hampden Park football ground where his teenage years were fairly typical, as he grew up with a passion for the sport and especially Celtic FC.

Like much of Britain, Bobby's childhood was sound-tracked by The Beatles and The Rolling Stones, but of later on he recalls: "When I was ten or eleven, I would hear T Rex, David Bowie, Gary Glitter; glam rock, I kind of loved all that." Having developed this fondness for glam, his tastes then advanced to the sterner sounds of Thin Lizzy and The Clash - two acts renowned for their maverick tendencies. Listening to him discuss his formative years, particularly via a series of throwaway remarks, it's a fair assumption that Bobby nowadays likes to give the impression that his youth was nothing short of anarchic, but the more likely scenario was that he was a quiet boy who found fascination in music.

"When I was a kid I'd buy *ZigZag* and *NME*," he told the latter in 1999, "and I'd read interviews with bands like Public Image Ltd, The Jam and The Clash, and they'd talk about people like Can, Captain Beefheart, Love, Miles Davis and John Coltrane..." Following such lines, young Bobby's knowledge of music from bygone eras expanded rapidly, it was something he would lean on in later years, citing these artists as both influences and inspirations. An interest in music has long since shielded young people from potentially hazardous lifestyles and certainly during the many difficult times ahead Bobby's appetite was such that it would always help him focus.

The very cult of rock 'n' roll has never been just about the music; the behaviour, attitude and, more often than not, the offensive intent of the performers holds an allure. During Britain's developing punk scene, many young, impressionable music fans suddenly came face-to-face with the possibility that they could escape the boredom of their everyday lives. Kids everywhere bought cheap guitars, learned how to strum three chords and formed a band. It was fun, liberating and easy, and it captivated the teenage Bobby Gillespie almost overnight.

He understood the appeal of punk loud and clear, and couldn't have been more excited about it, as he told *Sounds* in 1990: "Punk music gave me the courage to be myself and I met Alan through that. I'd always thought that there must be people who think like me and when I heard 'God Save The Queen' I thought, 'great! there's somebody else who hates The Queen as much as I do'. It's simple, but that's the power of rock 'n' roll!" By discovering punk Bobby realised that any lack of musical talent need not be a handicap; enthusiasm and attitude were more important.

Of his time at King's Park Secondary School Bobby recalls: "It was weird because I was in good classes for English, Art and History, but I was in remedial classes for Maths and Science, anything like that. In remedial, there's no teacher. They put you in a room and throw the key away." At school Bobby first became aware of Alan McGee and Robert Young. The three of them would soon drift together through music.

Much to the chagrin of his father, Alan McGee had his sights set on becoming a musician, though luckily he soon realised that he was perhaps more likely to be a success releasing records rather than making them.

Bobby first recognised Alan as a boy with taste, as he had a reputation around school for being a music lover. In October 1976 Thin Lizzy performed at Glasgow's Apollo Theatre and Bobby phoned the older boy asking if he wanted to go. "The way I met Alan was he'd be the only other guy in the area on the way back from Clash gigs on the train" is how he's since put it.

Either way the friendship between the two would remain intact for more than twenty-five years, during which time Alan would often refer to Bobby as his soulmate or brother. As they became friends, it was perhaps inevitable that they too should want to indulge in the spreading plague of punk, and the defining inspiration arrived after Alan caught a show on local radio. McGee was motivated by the announcement that a local band called The Drains were looking for new members. There mustn't have been any mention of a required level of ability, as he wasted no time applying, coming to the rescue of fifteen-year old Andrew Innes.

Innes had been a ball boy for the locally celebrated Scotland v England match at Hampden in '76. Like Bobby and Alan, he was also taken in by the 'anyone can do it' ethos of punk and refreshingly, he could really play guitar; such was his ability that Alan was moved to try and learn what he could from his new friend about the bass. Vague recollections from early 1978 reveal that Andrew changed the name of The Drains to Captain Scarlet And The Mysterons when Bobby joined on vocals. Although Bobby privately fancied himself as a percussionist, he couldn't sing or play anything at all, but it was hardly of any matter, as he was at last having a great time.

"You go round to your friend's house and try and play an instrument, you know, just mess about," he says, naively. The romance of friends getting together like this had always been part of the appeal of rock 'n' roll, and here were Bobby Gillespie, Alan McGee and Andrew Innes, the latest in a very long line of teenagers who dreamt of making it big. Back in the real world, Bobby left school with three 'O' Levels, while Alan, having grown tired of running as a trainee electrician, was soon holding down a day job with British Rail.

Still, Alan and Andrew were more dedicated than Bobby at this stage and during the next couple of years they liaised on both an early version of long forgotten synth darlings H_2O and the more prosperous Newspeak. By the summer of 1980, Andrew and Newspeak singer Jack Reilly had become disillusioned with Glasgow and convinced Alan to move to London.

It was surprising to many who knew eighteen-year old Andrew, who was rather inhibited by nature, that he could leave college and move hundreds of miles to a strange city, but such was his ambition that Alan felt compelled to follow his lead, as he says: "Me and Innes, being spiky characters, were either going to beat each other up or bond. We were geeky characters, outsiders. We liked being in London but the rest of the band were missing Glasgow and moved back." Once they were humbly squashed together in Tooting Bec, it was Jack Reilly who gathered he'd made a mistake and returned to Scotland. It was the end of Newspeak.

With a reference from their Glasgow counterparts, London's British Rail employed Alan where he quickly excelled. Alan persuaded his girlfriend to move down with him, yet she apparently still had doubts about the likelihood of him settling into a routine domestic life knowing that Andrew was determined to make it as a musician. As real life often gets in the way of dreams, nothing happened overnight.

Alan is loath to discuss their early musical endeavours in any detail, admitting only that while not especially great, their efforts were all more or less the same as any of the other kids' attempts at the dawn of the 80s. "I'm amazed we got through it actually," he admits, "we were mixed up kids suddenly in London where we didn't know anyone. I suppose you have less fear when you're younger; I remember thinking it was an exciting new beginning. I wanted to be the bass player in a top band and it was like Innes was showing me the way to go." London was more liberal than Glasgow; something they discovered as soon as they arrived, it was dangerous too, but as young musicians in search of the next great British rock band, it was definitely the place to be. Bobby was unable and unwilling to follow, but he stayed in close contact, visiting when he could, and has since stated that he was pleased, not jealous, when he heard they'd actually started to get somewhere.

With drummer Mark Jardim, Alan and Andrew formed The Laughing Apple and had three cheaply pressed singles released on labels they set up with sponsorship money from Govan CND. Their catchy guitar pop received favourable reviews from those who heard it around London, and for a time it seemed as if they might really get on their way. As early as 1981 the seeds were sown that over the next three years would germinate into one of the most important independent record labels of the decade.

Sadly though, progress was halted when Andrew fell ill with hepatitis and returned to Glasgow. Then Alan almost lost his life when the tour van spun out of control and crashed following a date up in Scotland. These unlucky breaks saw the pair lose momentum and they decided to take their time before considering any further musical plans. Alan married and got ever more comfortable with British Rail, but soon afterwards, those distressing thoughts of wasted youth that only become apparent to most people in midlife began to irk him in his early twenties. Inevitably, Alan wanted to express himself again. If he wasn't to be a musician because of low morale and general lack of talent, then he'd do the next best thing, so along with Laughing Apple fan Jerry Thackray he started a rock fanzine called *Communication Blur.*

While punk as a genre of music had hardly been a success in every conventional sense of the word, it had proved inspirational to a generation of young people who otherwise wouldn't have had the courage to do anything. The brash and carefree attitudes had spread to everyone from aspiring writers to filmmakers; just about anyone who realised that music was only a minor element of what was essentially a no holds barred approach to freedom of expression. In the early 80s inexpensive new fanzines appeared every week benefiting all kinds of young bands and helped likeminded individuals to interact. *Communication Blur* was impressive, which for obvious reasons plugged The Laughing Apple singles and especially helped revitalise Alan's enthusiasm for live music, so much so that before long he hired a small venue and put on concerts by unsigned young bands. It was a particularly bold scheme for a twenty-two-year-old with no experience, but his enthusiasm made these relative shortcomings look minor.

"I started a club," he recalls, "I didn't do it to make money, I just didn't know anyone in London at the time, and I thought I'd meet people if I started putting on bands I liked." Although by no means alone, Alan found the expense of acquiring a suitable venue that met safety regulations too great, but because he had a strong will, he found a way. To partner his fanzine, The Communication Club opened in Autumn 1982 and Alan quickly realised that if any of the young bands he was putting on had a record deal, then it was often a very poor one. Whilst pondering with his ambitions, the club sadly proved too expensive, forcing him to close down after little more than two months. Yet it had been a great creative success and, proud of what he'd achieved, he saved up for six months or so and with the help of a considerable tax rebate tried again, this time opening a venue called The Living Room.

Smaller than The Communication Club, The Living Room was a cosy venue situated above a pub where rock fans could be relied upon to come down, watch the bands and indulge in lively banter, the subject of which was often the lack of quality guitar acts during the whole synth pop era. In this unlikely setting unknown bands would play sensational shows and Alan soon managed to fill the room on word of mouth alone and before he knew it, he was sitting on a passionate community of rock 'n' roll fans. Feeling immensely proud when the club began to make a real profit, Alan took the plunge and borrowed a thousand pounds from his bank and put out a single, quitting British Rail soon afterwards.

McGee's ambitions for a record label were modest to say the least, he wanted to provide an outlet for people like him and ultimately give young bands an opportunity to see their work on vinyl. Talking to *Select* magazine he later explained that: "In an unconscious way, I was trying to merge psychedelia with punk rock. I was obsessed by bands like The Creation and Syd Barrett, but I also loved Joy Division and PiL. The music scene was dominated by manufactured pop. Me and Bobby would sit saying how much we hated everything. We had all these great ideas, like water bombing pop stars..."

Evidently there were never any long term plans; if Alan managed to put out just one single then it would be an achievement, two would be really gathering steam and three would be incredible. His professed aim was to provide a voice for the disaffected and, if it all fell apart before it started then at least he could say he tried. Alan called the business Creation, after one of his favourite bands.

With the Laughing Apple finished, Jerry Thackray's alias 'The Legend' has the honour of being Creation's first ever release with the single '73 in 83'. With his girlfriend Christine, Andrew Innes had formed

Revolving Paint Dream; their 'Flowers In The Sky' was the second, and with partner Dick Green, Alan himself dusted down his bass playing skills in Biff Bang Pow, their 'Fifty Years Of Fun' completing the label's hat-trick of releases.

Up in Glasgow Bobby Gillespie had kept reasonably busy. He'd designed the covers for The Laughing Apple singles and had them printed along with issues of *Communication Blur*, as he'd been employed at a print factory since leaving school. Despite the post having its benefits, Bobby didn't last long in the job as he came to hate both the conventional hours and day-to-day boredom of a labour he's since called 'a slow death'. However the nightlife was much more to his taste and Bobby had already begun to make a name for himself around the city. For a short while he was a roadie for Clare Grogan's Altered Images, who at first glance didn't seem to make ideal company but at least he was involved in music, which left him relatively content. There was another band who Bobby got to know called The Wake, who he assisted in several roles both in the studio and on tour, notably opening for the infant Joy Division offspring New Order.

Joy Division have accurately been described as a devastating cross between The Doors and Nirvana. Featuring the original, self-taught guitar style of their future singer Bernard Sumner and the distinctive lead bass lines of Peter Hook, their music had had a great impact on teenage Bobby; who later went on to declare that the only reason he became a singer was because of Sumner, and that his future bassist later had a 'Heart And Soul' tattoo done because of the Joy Division song. But it was with a touring mate of The Wake in mid 1983 that Bobby felt the inspiration to again be in a band, the same feeling he'd had when he first heard Andrew Innes play those punk anthems more than five years before.

In a local scout hut, aspiring folk guitarist Jim Navajo Beattie began to make noise with his instrument and additional fuzz pedals. Bobby Gillespie would scream and bang on dustbin lids creating an almighty racket that apparently should have sounded like songs by The Byrds and The Velvet Underground. The name 'Primal Scream' was chosen for this venture because it sounded brilliant; it was a term coined by Dr Arthur Janov's famed book on psychotherapy treatment and would always carry certain implications for their music. More than once the tag would prove gloriously misleading.

When word reached Alan, he invited Bobby and Jim

down to play The Living Room as a twosome. Gillespie and Beattie did perform in some way, likely with the help of a beat box, but whether or not officially as Primal Scream is still a matter of conjecture, as with a hazy recollection Bobby later mentioned that: "The first ever Primal Scream gig was at the Bungalow Bar in Paisley, we supported The Laughing Apple. Only one song in the set was ours, and I remember it was just total noise. That wasn't a real gig, it was a joke. There wasn't any shape to it." Still, despite the blurriness, Alan's club is probably the safest assumption to be the location of Primal Scream's live debut - although no one has been able to get specific.

As Primal Scream were in business and releasing records by mid '85, Bobby's first press exposure arrived accordingly and of the very early days he told fanzines and music papers up and down the land that it started as just total noise; smashing things up, with any apparent melody just purely coincidental, telling *ZigZag:* "we used to make noises, then we learnt to play guitars, then we learnt to write songs, and we quite liked it, and we thought, 'we'll try and get a group, try and get records out' and things like that." Meanwhile he told *Jamming!* that: "When Primal Scream started, all Jim and I used to do was make tapes of noise, then we progressed to writing tunes around bass riffs, and then we started writing pop songs." When they were confident enough with their first handful of compositions, getting some of them recorded properly was the next obvious step. Leaning on Alan's generosity they nominated a new, 60s pop influenced number called 'The Orchard' to be their first single.

One of Bobby's friends, Judith Boyle, was brought in to contribute violin to Primal Scream's first real studio session. In later years, Bobby claimed that he was suffering with a cold when it was time to record his vocals and asked her to duet with him, hoping she'd disguise his inadequacies. It was rumoured that Bobby found Judith's voice so impressive that he took singing more seriously from then on, attempting to croon like a girl. It's ironic that right from the start of his career Bobby's desire for absolute perfection, in both recording and mixing, proved to be hugely problematic, as 'The Orchard', in its definitive form at least, remains a lost treasure as, deeply dissatisfied with the result, Bobby and Jim staunchly refused it any exposure, commenting later that they purposely destroyed the tape. Creation Records, not for the last time, were left waiting.

Further compositions like 'Hollow' and 'Leaves' came together as they become something of a mainstay around Glasgow's band scene. Nick Lowe co-ran The Candy Club, a venue that Bobby and Jim frequented in the hope of meeting like-minded people. It was a place for young bands to get up and play and accordingly it was inundated with demo tapes, including those from a young group who had called themselves everything from The Poppy Seeds to The Death Of Joey before settling on Daisy Chain after they correctly assumed that bookers had tired of hearing from them. They would develop into arguably the most important street band of the decade.

Brothers William and Jim Reid hailed from East Kilbride, a suburb of south Glasgow, where they were making every effort to escape the stultifying life predicted for their generation - a life that had begun to assume depressing reality. Along with their pushy mate Douglas Hart, their love of classic Beach Boys style pop and punk noise terrorism saw them inspiringly combine the two genres to a startlingly original and powerful effect. Their sound was akin to the beauty of The Velvet Underground beneath an incredible wall of distorted guitar that merged into something rebellious and wonderfully new. One of their earliest recordings was sent to Nick Lowe at The Candy Club, who casually mentioned to Bobby

Gillespie that he might like it. He did.

Bobby quickly contacted Douglas Hart, as he later recalled: "I phoned the number on the tape and spent two hours talking to Dougie; total strangers talking about the books, films and records we loved. It was great because me and my mates had felt isolated, we thought we were the only guys around who liked what we liked."

With Douglas on bass, the Reids' band was now called The Jesus And Mary Chain, and Bobby was certain that he could offer not only a record deal, but live dates in London and even some media exposure, as because of Alan's persistence, some of the city's sharpest young music journalists were now conveniently propping up The Living Room's bar. Although he could hardly afford to put another band in the studio, Alan was quickly learning the ropes of the business and once he saw The Mary Chain perform a gloriously sloppy set, he followed suit and made a desperate attempt to release them. When they were finally convinced, Alan put them in the studio in September 1984 to record their debut single 'Upside Down'.

Murray Dalglish held the drumming responsibilities for The Mary Chain, but as he had no creative input to the band, it was assumed by all that he would expect only minimal royalties and exposure on their forthcoming tour. Yet now that they had a single coming out Dalglish was unhappy and because of his attitude was soon told by the Reid brothers that he was no longer required. The hunt for a replacement was on, which just had to be Bobby, despite the fact that he couldn't drum to save his fresh-faced life. He still accepted the offer with glee, laughing as he told *The Guardian* sixteen years later: "I was speeding out of my head one night and the drummer didn't turn up, so I went on stage, stood behind the drum kit and did my Mo Tucker bit. Never drummed before in my life, but it worked."

Jim Beattie soon became concerned about the future of Primal Scream, whose first truly official concert was opening for The Jesus And Mary Chain at Glasgow's The Venue on the 11 October. "My first gig with The Chain was my first gig with The Scream, simultaneously," Bobby recalled, "the poster was a picture from *If...*; there was Malcolm McDowell holding a hand grenade demanding, 'Whose Side Are You On?'"

On the night, Bobby sang in Primal Scream for fifteen minutes or so, then returned to the stage to drum with The Mary Chain, though he did little more than whack the high hat and look cool. The Mary Chain's next date however, in Islington two weeks later, was reviewed by the *NME* and mentioned the drummer junking his stool, grinning like an idiot and smashing out with extra force. It was one of their earliest write-ups, which just happened to set alight the touch paper.

In the wake of punk came an incredible increase in the number of independent record labels. As thoroughly documented elsewhere, the meaning of independent in terms of music often means different things to different people, but perhaps a conventional example is that of Rough Trade Records and its unique distribution system. What had started out as a handful of store owners agreeing on a whim to supply every street record they were asked, had by 1984 grown into an empire that was the envy of several majors that had noted its efficient methods without compromising the punk ethos behind it.

Rough Trade began as a dusty record shop in London's West End in the mid 70s by a passionate Cambridge graduate named Geoff Travis. The shop sold self-financed singles by artists usually unable to get rid of surplus stock, and word quickly spread that perhaps 'indies' didn't have to grovel to the big boys to circulate their product after all. As the dealings escalated Rough Trade grew into a label, as Travis's experimental distribution network had proved a surprising success with many like minded labels and store owners around Britain. Even Joy Division's absurdly stubborn home Factory, in faraway Manchester, were suitably onboard to see their seminal debut LP *Unknown Pleasures* sufficiently get round the UK in '79. By '83 Rough Trade had grown strong enough to get new arrivals The Smiths on *Top Of The Pops* and see Travis in negotiations with Warner Brothers about the setting up of a pioneering new 'major indie' style company.

Alan McGee had hardly got rich from Rough Trade taking on The Laughing Apple records, but the impression Creation had made with its first releases was definite progress. By the time of The Jesus And Mary Chain's first record, Creation's eleventh, keen young *NME* writers were helpfully spreading the gospel and the breakthrough arrived as 'Upside Down' grew into arguably the most important indie single of the mid 80s.

Critics were stunned by its disordered sound, and for the Mary Chain and the extremely slender Creation Records it was an absolutely phenomenal success; eventually selling an incredible fifty thousand copies across Britain. Alan remembers not being able to meet the demand and, quickly noting their potential, he encouraged the Reids to extrovert themselves and look worthy of the press attention, which by early '85 had reached fever pitch. Descriptions like 'The Most Exciting Band in Seven Years' were commonplace, as the single had by then - the Factory New Order hit 'Blue Monday' aside - provoked the most widespread opinion from any new alternative record since the explosion of punk. McGee called it quits at The Living Room as The Mary Chain's ball began to roll at phenomenal pace.

Unsurprisingly they attracted huge interest from a number of major record labels. Blanco Y Negro, the afore mentioned 'major indie' just set up by Geoff Travis with Warner Brothers' money, quickly offered a multi-album contract that included massive distribution and strong promotion. It was a proposition that Creation couldn't hope to match, so it was fairly inevitable that Jim and William would make the switch to the bigger label. There was little acrimony from Alan over the move, partly because he never actually had them under contract, but mostly because he would continue to manage them and subsequently learn about how majors operate.

Of course McGee noted the way profit was considered under threat by artists expressing themselves but, at the same time, understood that because of the regulations they enforced, majors would eventually have the necessary funds that the independents didn't. It's highly unlikely that The Jesus And Mary Chain would have been initially picked up by a major, what with all their unconventional use of distortion and feedback, but since they'd now critically and commercially proved themselves, Warners swiftly moved in and presented them with an opportunity that Creation was in no position to equal. The band couldn't possibly have developed any further on Alan's label and that simply came down to money. Unlike Creation, Blanco Y Negro could afford the fifteen thousand pounds or so it would cost for The Mary Chain to record a full length album. For the band, it was the obvious next step.

Despite all the attention, Jim and William Reid were still frustratingly shy characters and, as their band was really taking off, it was bizarre that the press were portraying them as a pair of thugs who could barely strum beginner's chords. This theory soon proved laughable however as their dedication to the cause became total. Having picked up and moved into London bedsits, their determination to be as good a band as they could was propelled by Alan, who saw them as his ticket to stardom, as both an eccentric manager and PR agent; one with an ear for an alternative to the standard rock fairs that toured the Smoke. He booked them a concert at the North London Polytechnic, a small venue frequented by students who had heeded the advice of the music press that fans should reserve tickets in advance. The promoters and scarce security, who unwisely decided to admit people on a first-come-first-served basis, would not have a routine evening.

Firstly, there was trouble outside the venue when scores of angry fans, many in possession of valid tickets, were turned away as the venue had already exceeded its capacity. Bobby and Douglas Hart attempted to kick open the doors to let people in and the police were called. Then, once the show got underway, a technical fault turned the set into little more than a ten minute howl of feedback which moved the drunken band to leave the stage in disgust. Feeling short-changed, angry members of the audience then began to vandalise the stage and steal the band's equipment. Things got rapidly out of hand when the police arrived, as the looters fought amongst themselves using bottles and cans as weapons; eventually causing more than seven thousand pounds worth of damage to the hall. Having escaped the venue with their lives intact, the group's blasé statement declared that they were putting excitement back into rock 'n' roll and that the promoters would have to bear the consequences.

Although an isolated mass riot, it cemented the reputation of The Jesus And Mary Chain as the most notorious attraction on the guitar underground. The shrewd Alan McGee saw his chance and began to glibly spread all sorts of rumours, rumours that the band did little to deny. The fracas at the North London Polytechnic, it was claimed, was instigated by the band's management solely for publicity, a claim that, if true, worked an absolute sensation. The rest of the tour also turned out to be anarchic enough to force several promoters to cancel and soon everywhere that The Jesus And Mary Chain managed to book there were fears of disturbances and concern for audience safety. The press, needless to say, lapped it up. Suddenly expectations for The Mary Chain towered and nothing less than a twenty-four carat classic of a debut LP would satisfy the press, or their mammoth group of hooligan followers.

Maybe they weren't selling quite as many records as Simple Minds, but as part of The Jesus And Mary Chain, Bobby Gillespie turned seemingly overnight from a quiet young man to rock 'n' roll brat. He was only the drummer, but many close to him noticed a blinding change in his personality. On one occasion, during an interview with Jim and William for a Belgian television programme, Bobby was seen in the background practically having sex with a girl on a sofa. Quick to defend himself, Bobby announced: "Part of that is, I like girls, and sometimes, if you want to go and get a lot of girls, then you should. If girls like you and you like girls, then there's no reason you shouldn't have sex with them. I don't think it's a big deal. It just happens to be that because you're in a rock 'n' roll band, people say, 'oh, the rock myth..'.'"

Whilst performing, Bobby preferred not to sit on the customary drum stool but rather stand behind his two piece kit looking completely oblivious to everything happening around him. He banged away - his specialised technique was apparently to hit the drums, and then hit them again - often completely out of time from the rest of the band which in an accidental kind of way seemed to compliment the guitar hailstorm that raged around him. Dressed in black with his adorable fringe elegantly swept into an overgrown nerdy style, he looked uncannily like a young Mo Tucker - the drummer from his heroes The Velvet Underground, and in comparison to the hardly magnetic Reid brothers, it was assumed by many that it was actually Bobby who was the real focal point of the group.

Although enjoying himself hugely with The Mary

Chain, Bobby was determined to keep Primal Scream going as he felt he could express himself better as a frontman. Though he could barely sing, he appreciated the opportunity to embrace the stage in a way no drummer could. He had become the drummer with The Mary Chain as a favour to Jim and William and even the fact that their band had come a very long way in a short space of time never clouded the casual nature of that agreement. The Reid brothers never lost sight of this, as Bobby frequently told them that he would help out while he could, but in the long term it was likely that they'd have to find a more permanent sticksman as Primal Scream developed into a serious concern.

Alongside Jim Beattie three mates had since joined: drummer Tom McGurk, tambourinist Martin St John and bassist Robert Young completed the first Primal Scream line-up and helped provide the essential gang mentality that was every bit as important to a young band as musical ability. This five-piece recorded the first Primal Scream single 'All Fall Down' backed with 'It Happens' released on Creation in May. Alan says: "The vocals were done in one take. Bobby takes too long over them, he's totally paranoid and redoes everything about a thousand times, a total perfectionist." Listening to it, it was clear that by now

Bobby and Jim had developed a distinct affection for the chiming sound of the Rickenbacker guitar. In the next two years they developed the sound to an extent that would characterise the first real era of Primal Scream; they were young hopefuls, yet to make the record that justified their ambition as neither song was out of the ordinary - a view with which the critics largely concurred.

Speaking to Neil Taylor, the *NME* journalist who first championed The Mary Chain, Bobby announced: "I don't want people to think 'oh that's the guy from The Jesus And Mary Chain, better check the single out', because that's just rubbish, it's second hand. I want people to appreciate us for what we are and not who our friends are. Remember, I was in this group before I joined the Mary Chain, and the only reason I joined them was because they needed a drummer and I could keep time."

In-between working with both bands, Bobby had even begun organising entertainment for the young people of Glasgow. One night every two weeks, he put on an evening at a club called *Splash One*, where live bands played and Bobby managed to indulge in his passion for classic and alternative pop as a hopeful DJ. Explaining his reasoning, he later complained that there just wasn't anywhere in Glasgow to see bands or hear that kind of music. Though the brief venture wasn't a huge success, Bobby's enthusiasm was there for all to see. It was an admirable display of passion from a young man who, to raise the old hooray cliché, even then seemed a candidate to leave a positive mark on independent British music.

The Mary Chain briefly visited Europe and towards the end of the year even America and Canada where the reaction was predictably muted. For Bobby, just to rock and oppose the New Romantic fashions far from Johnny Rotten was more than enough. At home he awaited reaction to the album they'd recently recorded at London's Southern Studios.

Featuring Bobby on drums, *Psychocandy* was released through Warners that winter and surpassed all expectations, being hailed as the freshest album of the year by critics right across the board. One would have thought that such acclaim would be enough to convince Bobby to forget Primal Scream, but as The Mary Chain primarily belonged to songwriters Jim and William, he knew that any creative ambitions he had wouldn't be realised as their drummer. As they grew, Bobby's situation was becoming intolerable. At the start of 1986, when asked to learn the drums properly and commit fully to The Mary Chain, he

declined, later explaining: "I love The Jesus And Mary
Chain, but they asked me to join the group, and I had
to make a decision; with them I would have just been a
drummer, with no real artistic input. The Mary Chain
is just Jim and William, you know, I loved playing with
them, it was the best time of my life." Bobby then
amicably left the employ of the Reid brothers, leaving
him free to concentrate on his own band.

While Primal Scream was merely one moderately
well-received single old, the other band, the one Bobby
had been busying his weekends with, happened to be
just about the most exciting thing to happen to Britain's
sterile rock scene in more than half a decade. The Mary
Chain were clearly the more prosperous career option
for Gillespie but his decision to opt for Primal Scream
instead was a display of boldness that would have had
many pondering missed opportunities. Yet as his
songwriting with Jim Beattie was coming along,
especially now that he'd seen up close that it really
could be done, there was a certain inevitability about
him wanting to better himself on centre stage. Working
for yourself is always cooler than working for someone
else and, as previously mentioned, he couldn't take
himself seriously as a drummer. He wasn't good at it;
that's not to say he was a gifted singer either, though
that hardly mattered. Bobby couldn't sing, but he

wanted to, and that, as any of punk's children will testify, is more than half the battle.

sonic flower groove

Glasgow, famously balanced by a tender sectarian divide, was as tough a city as could be found in mid 1980s Britain and it was perhaps only natural that an ambitious young band should inherit some of the assertive arrogance that slipped from the mighty River Clyde and the working class communities that surrounded it. Bobby Gillespie and Jim Beattie were proud to have made progress in their plan to escape a lifestyle that many of their peers were sadly falling into; one that would often lead to crime, drugs and in many cases premature death. No doubt via his experiences with The Mary Chain, Bobby in particular had realised the value of publicity and long after he'd made it once declared that: "If you come from Glasgow you're a leftist, it's the way we look at the world."

Unquestionably the city was full of leftists, tough talking young bands, many of whom were already in the slipstream of The Mary Chain. But there certainly weren't many who were desperate to sound as delicate as Love or The Byrds. Accordingly, writers weren't slow to knock Primal Scream as immature boys acting way out of their league. Their single was declared soft;

their sound was too clean, too romantic - it had no right to stem from such a murky home town.

With momentum gathering following a short nationwide tour, the songwriting was well under way with the sessions entirely dominated by Bobby and Jim. 'Slow Death Song' and 'Tomorrow Ends Today' were two new compositions that sat alongside such numbers as 'Imperial', 'Aftermath' and 'Sometimes Everything'. This period of writing was the pair's most productive yet; indeed they came up with an excess of new songs, and although many of them would never see the light of day, the sounds nonetheless confirmed either their admirable knowledge of rock history or, as the cynics put it, their status as simply no more than weedy 60s plagiarists.

They persevered, determined to make a go of a career in pop. After all, with the contacts they had, there was every reason to expect that, like The Mary Chain, they too could bore journalists and terrorise promoters on their way to making a similar impact. But all that though; their label, the lively gig circuit and the press; existed in London, not Glasgow, some four hundred miles away. Visiting Alan and the increasing numbers in his social circle gave Primal Scream plenty of reason to relocate but it was a question of desire. While they were enjoying themselves; travelling and honing their craft, the early performances were at best receiving just nods of approval, rather than the rave reviews Alan was busy spreading to the critics who'd been overwhelmed by The Mary Chain. This was wasn't surprising as the shows seldom lasted longer than twenty minutes and as a result Primal Scream were often labelled idle, with little substance to support their boasts of greatness.

Early on they were writing songs that were of a style, substance, and often alarmingly brief length that only they wanted. It was pop music; entertainment that should provoke an upbeat feeling in the listener to help them get through the day that little bit easier. There would always be those who felt compelled to investigate the art further but the sentimental nature of their early compositions was bred out of their genuine passion for top sounding pop; they were, first and foremost, fans, and as the filthy business was creeping up on them, that certainly helped.

Visually, the first full version of Primal Scream; Bobby, Jim, Robert Young, Martin St John, Tom McGurk and new rhythm guitarist Paul Harte, brought to mind many of the 60s psychedelic groups from America's West Coast, as leather was the dominant look with silk shirts and round sunglasses part of the uniform. It was an image that didn't sit too well with certain locals: "You can walk down the street wearing leather trousers - which to me is inoffensive," declared Bobby, "but I was on the train the other day, and I walked by these guys who were obviously in the army, and they were blowing me kisses saying 'come here darling.' I felt like turning round and saying 'I can't wait until you get posted to Northern Ireland and the IRA blows your head off'."

Clearly, the singer didn't pay too much attention to what other people thought of how he dressed but sensibly took care to develop the band's music. As the first signs of their fascination with jangly guitars were coming to prominence, the fact that they wore leather was somewhat surprising as, in rock speak, they just didn't look how they sounded. They hadn't quite got the image to match their sound, it could easily have become an issue that they'd have to address, but for now though, and despite the jibes, leather was most definitely in.

At least by an increasing number of young people, Primal Scream were becoming the subject of genuine affection. At shows, floppy Bobby haircuts started to appear which if nothing else ensured a good atmosphere and a healthy queue for autographs by the stage exit. While appreciating such adoration, the band wanted more than giggly fanzine writers giving them the type of reviews they honestly felt they deserved. Even if they were hardly in line for a *Rolling Stone* cover, they nonetheless felt hurt by the ignorance of the dominant press, while national radio exposure was proving even harder to come by. The latter's resistance was only occasionally cracked when the odd jock was brave enough to sneak the single onto the airwaves and even then it was nearly always at a pretty useless hour. Understandably Bobby wasn't happy, complaing: "This group should make it on its own merits but it's so difficult getting radio play - too many DJs just sling indie records in the bin. It's not that I think· we should be given hours of radio play, it's just that we should have access to compete on equal terms, with those records that so seemingly get automatic airplay. Our songs are melodic, they're accessible - all we're asking for is a chance."

The quest for stardom was always Bobby's prerogative and the hardships that accompanied it seemed to pile up as he explained in interview after interview that 'when' his band made it, it would be on their own terms without having benefited from the apparently hip status of being on a small independent label. He correctly claimed that it made no difference who was paying for their tapes and that they shouldn't be saddled with any reputation to do with anything other than how their records sounded. "I think that new bands in this country are choked even before they're born," he grumbled, "there's a lot of new, really good pop groups in Britain who are totally ignored as a result of American rock and inverted racism on the part of journalists..." Those remarks earned sympathy at the *NME* which shared his concern. The paper was plotting a fight back for young British bands and Primal Scream would ironically feature in a way that would hang like an albatross round their necks for years.

Trying to maintain a patient attitude after initial exposure is understandably difficult for a young band. Yet although having vinyl out and garnering the odd national review was a fine achievement, it was still a very long way from comforting success. In reality, Primal Scream were indistinguishable from millions of other fresh hopefuls, all aching for that combination of hard work and luck to present them with that killer exposure. It was never this difficult for The Mary Chain, Bobby must have surely noted and inevitably tensions arose. With standards and ambitions set almost too high, rhythm guitarist Paul Harte was replaced by Stewart May. It was a minor line-up change, the like of which would frequently occur throughout the next decade or so, as Primal Scream became something of a revolving door behind their obsessive lead singer.

Because Alan was generally busy with the Reid Brothers and with there being an overall lack of funds at Creation, it was a whole year following 'All Fall Down' before Primal Scream could release the follow up single 'Crystal Crescent'. But it was an eighty-five second sprint through the most adorable melodic pop called 'Velocity Girl' included on the record that first brought them to the attention of the public.

1986 was to be a quiet year for press-sponsored independent bands; while The Smiths would put out the album of the year, the Stephen Street produced *The Queen Is Dead*, the usually reliable New Order for instance could only manage their rather indifferent *Brotherhood* LP. Staunchly ignoring the influx of foreign acts worth fussing over and in the hope of creating a new, solely domestic movement, the *NME* unleashed its giveaway *C86* tape in May, on which 'Velocity Girl' was the lead track.

A sensation of a pop tune, why it was never chosen as a bona fide single in its own right is as curious a question as any in the story of Primal Scream. While 'Crystal Crescent' was initially thought of as the stronger of the two, the heavy emphasis they subsequently placed on it resulted in an over produced failure of an A side, and they soon realised, as Bobby graciously said at the time: "It's ironic, we love pop music so much, but we can't even get the record right. I suppose it's good in some ways to make such a mistake - we're still learning."

But in the days when records had two sides, the release was supremely championed by the *NME* who loved its companion 'Velocity Girl' so much that when discussing it, they went so far as to virtually predict the future of British pop. In hindsight, even taken quite literally, this proved an uncannily accurate prophesy, as a band of similar genetics from Manchester called The Stone Roses were so impressed by 'Velocity Girl' that they would, quite blatantly, rework the song into a genuine indie classic. According to the pop professors, their 1989 single 'Made Of Stone' opened the flood gates for the torrent of proud soundalikes that would dominate Britain's music scene some ten years after 'Crystal Crescent' and 'Velocity Girl'; it was as if Primal Scream had planted a seed....

Not that any of this mattered at the time. The exposure guaranteed by *C86* - much the press hype of the year - one would have thought, would have been very much appreciated. Yet Bobby was unsure of the reputation this dropped on his band, clearly believing that being generalised with such company just wasn't fitting, as he told that very publication three years later: "We never had anything in common with those bands. We got a phone call asking us to be on an *NME* compilation and we said okay. If you look at my record collection, you'll see I have no time for that sort of stuff, independent music is pretty inferior; they can't play their instruments and they can't write songs... I don't like putting other bands down, it just looks like sour grapes because they sell more than us."

Nonetheless, Primal Scream were going to make what would 'surely' be some great records and that alone would be what they'd be commended for, Bobby liked to think, not a review in a music paper that only a year previously was largely indifferent towards them. Looking back, it's worth noting that by the next decade when their profile had risen, virtually all the other acts included on the *C86* never got much further and have since been doomed to cult mid 80s status forever.

In the summer, a longer version of 'Velocity Girl' was recorded but like so much material from this era it received little exposure. The original however still remains one of the best loved songs in their entire catalogue. Future friends The Manic Street Preachers recorded a cover some years later; underlining Primal

Scream's significance as an underground act on what was then a genuine independent music scene. Not that Primal Scream would be a truly independent act for much longer, as on a small, but certainly significant scale, they were being hailed by more than one observer as perhaps, maybe, the Next Big Thing.

The Jesus And Mary Chain were said to represent the future of British independent music. Their arrival bucked the trend of new romanticism that had so callously snubbed the excitement of punk during the first half of the 80s. Accordingly Alan McGee was now able to sell other guitar acts to majors hoping to cash in on his ear for potential. Following the success and acclaim of The Mary Chain, and to a lesser degree Primal Scream's *C86* coverage, Alan was able set up a label with WEA, the European arm of Warner Brothers, who would fund the venture optimistically named Elevation.

This new label meant that Primal Scream were promoted to virtual major status after two small singles and would accordingly have the money to get a full-length album just right. Bobby Gillespie was twenty-four and finally a professional musician; suddenly his band were in the big time and the pressure was on, especially since Stephen Street was one of the producers who saw potential in their so far respectable recorded output. Street was hired to produce the debut LP at the renowned Rockfield Studios in rural Wales. Yet things didn't turn out as he would have liked.

For all the confidence in Primal Scream and all the abilities of Street, the fact that they were not disciplined with a big budget and inexperienced with even relatively simple arrangements ensured that the sessions were a huge failure. Bobby in particular was not able to perform. "Residential life did not suit us," Jim later explained, "and it got really bizarre, we started saying things like 'That cymbal's not right' and changing clothes for every solo. In fact, I threatened Stephen that I would play guitar in the nude!"

Bobby added: "The musicians weren't good enough and Street couldn't really handle it." Retorting to Danny Kelly, prior to the *NME* man's June '87 feature on the band, Street declared: "It was just incredible, like nothing I've ever experienced before. They're nice enough lads but you can't work with them. It all came to a head when I found myself arguing with Bobby about a solitary cymbal crash in a rhythm track; arguing fiercely for two solid hours."

Losing conviction and arguing over slight differences, they explained to Alan that things weren't working out but he was unable to offer any pity as this was no longer friendly free studio time but expensively funded by a huge company that expected the end product to be highly marketable. Under such weight of expectation, drummer Tom McGurk was dismissed which left many of the recording gaps to be filled by Dave Morgan, a Creation mate with The Weather Prophets. A line-up change of more importance was that of Andrew Innes replacing Stuart May by the new year.

As he'd known Bobby since he was a teenager, Andrew would hardly have problems settling in and his musical ability would benefit Primal Scream in the long term. After the acrimonious departure of Stephen Street, the new guitarist's enthusiasm was instrumental in motivating them to regroup and salvage what they could. The excellent 'Imperial' was recorded with Clive Langer and Colin Fairley at London's famous Abbey Road studios; a luxury that proved Warners had been suitably impressed to sink large amounts of money into the band. As the momentum had been lost, a decision was made to recover with live dates in the hope of creating a secure mental toughness before they returned to the studio.

Looking on, stage front right was Beattie and his glorious black and white Rickenbacker but between his co-star and the largely faceless rhythm section, was an individual whose responsibility it seemed was to bang a tambourine and nothing else. Having someone centre stage who basically did nothing wasn't exactly an accepted norm, as undoubtedly Martin St John was receiving more than his fair share of the limelight. He would dance around, bang away and absorb as much applause as any of them. It was perhaps the ultimate example of how, despite their expanding ability, belief was still held in higher regard than talent inside the Primal Scream faction. St John was an inspiring figure in the early days but after those successful dates in the summer of '87 he departed of his own accord and, unlike Paul Harte, who re-emerged as part of the touring entourage, he was never heard of again.

With an album still to deliver it was back to the drawing board, which in this case was at engineer Pat Collier's studio The Greenhouse. The new producer was Mayo Thompson, who eventually saw them through but, rather predictably, Bobby had little good to say about the second attempt at recording this first album: "We lost all spontaneity in the re-recording and it just about split up the group," he said. Not quite that drastic, but the album could scarcely be called a success.

Sonic Flower Groove, **as it was** officially titled, contained: 'Gentle Tuesday', 'Treasure Trip', 'May The Sun Shine Bright For You', 'Sonic Sister Love', 'Silent Spring', 'Imperial', 'Love You', 'Leaves', 'Aftermath' and 'We Go Down Slowly Rising'.

Opening track 'Gentle Tuesday' set the tone for the whole album with Jim's sharp and melodic guitar ringing throughout. The song's lyrics confirmed that it was indeed a conscious homage to the most elementary of all guitar pop. 'Treasure Trip' and 'May The Sun Shine Bright For You' were haunting offerings, giving the listener the impression of Bobby as the heartbroken poet, out of time in the present day, trying to reach the masses with a heartfelt plea for the medieval past. The most tongue-in-cheek song on the album, ironically the only cut that was saved from the sessions with Street, titled 'Love You', was a ballad that continued with the admirable Rickenbacker plucking backing a syrupy crescendo of sweet vocals.

Despite picking up acclaim from sections of the press that admired their brave attempt at Byrds-esque jangle pop, Primal Scream were far from pleased with their debut album and their whole status in general. They even went so far as to declare that they wanted the release cancelled; it was an aspiration Warners didn't grant. So like any other young band they went out and began playing the media game in earnest. That they weren't best pleased with the album made it all the more painful.

A video was made for the pre-released single 'Gentle Tuesday'. While they also gave a well refreshed performance of 'Imperial' and 'Silent Spring' on a short-lived TV show called *Full Scale Disaster,* during the recording of which they threatened to kill a cameraman if he made them look bad. The album was rush-released in September with drummer Gavin Skinner recruited for more live appearances, including a slot opening for New Order at the eight thousand capacity Wembley Arena, a memorable evening during which a drunken Bobby fell clean off the stage.

Into the new year founder member, lead guitarist and chief songwriter Jim Beattie quit. He played his last show as a member of Primal Scream at London's Camden Dingwalls in May 1988. Alan told the *NME*: "It was a completely amicable split, and I hope that any of Jim's future projects will still be released on Creation Records, I personally think he is one of the most talented guitarists to come out of the post-punk scene." It wasn't long though before the parting was revealed to be slightly more acrimonious. The guitarist said later that egos were running riot within the group, certain members of which were getting high opinions of their own importance that weren't to his liking. The endless touring had simply made the band no longer fun and the decision to move down to Brighton on the South Coast of England certainly didn't help Jim since he preferred to remain in Glasgow.

With singer Judith Boyle, Jim resurfaced in 1990 with a series of acclaimed demos. The name of his new outfit was Spirea X, the title of an old Primal Scream song that was included with 'Velocity Girl' on the twelve-inch 'Crystal Crescent'. When their debut album *Fireblade Skies* was talked up in the press, obviously in reference to his former band, Jim repeatedly claimed that everything would be better. Though a critical smash, the album didn't sell well and Spirea X split soon after. Little was heard from Beattie in the following years, but he and Boyle continued and by the mid 90s had formed Adventures In Stereo.

Since the split, contact between Beattie and the remaining members of Primal Scream has been minimal. Bobby has remained tight-lipped on what exactly happened.

Pitiful in sales, *Sonic Flower Groove* was less than a total success and the Elevation label folded soon afterwards. Warner Brothers showed no interest in any further work from Primal Scream or any of the other acts from Creation, to where the band returned to receive the type of liberties that were hardly tolerated by the major. It was very much a done deal, with little more professional commitment to Alan's label than there'd been on the handshake that first saw them on vinyl. The details of Primal Scream's official obligations to Creation were never publicly revealed; there was never any mention of fees, contracts or numbers of records expected; it's no doubt another case of McGee's casual loyalty to Bobby that stretched back to their days together as teenagers, when they would sit and endlessly debate the merits of classic and contemporary pop music.

Ironically, it was Bobby's passion for classic pop and his opinion of just what made a good record that made recording so difficult. The high standards he set for his own music made him extremely self-conscious during recording; he threw the weight of expectation on himself and the rest of the band, which resulted in much of the spontaneity that had promised so much being lost in a mire of self-doubt - a contrast to the swaggering displays of bravado put on for the press. The record had come together reluctantly from a band who tried too hard reaching for the stars, leaving it sounding too polished, and all too often quite uninspired.

Alan says: "Their LP didn't work because they just spent too long on it. Warners gave them a hundred and twenty-seven thousand pounds and they spent it all. The major music industry is based too much on the short-term thing; major record companies want hits instantly."

Amongst other things it was the expensive failure of the album that brought the end of Elevation. Yet nobody could deny the fact that the venture had put too much pressure on the relationship between Alan and his bands who had always been friends first and business partners second.

Following the stressful dealings with Warners, Alan admitted that juggling his managerial responsibilities to Primal Scream and his responsibilities to the big company were just too great. It didn't help either that he'd had all links cut with The Jesus And Mary Chain, who made it clear that their ambitions lay beyond what they thought his management skills could provide. Some reorganisation was clearly necessary, so when Primal Scream linked up with Brighton club regular Alex Nightingale, it was a most welcome move for all parties.

Nightingale, the son of BBC radio DJ Annie, enjoyed the sort of childhood that most kids could only dream of. Meeting an array of contemporary pop stars would have been an impossible dream for most children, yet Alex often found his home littered with the legends of British music. His mother knew everyone, so the fact that he would one day be employed in the industry was fairly inevitable. First becoming friends with Primal Scream and assuming the role of their booking agent, by the early 90s he had become their first full-time manager. After the debacle of Elevation, Alan regrouped to concentrate full time on Creation, a decision helped by the recent commercial success of The House Of Love and the arrival of a gang of beautiful noise makers called My Bloody Valentine. Thus Alex Nightingale became ever more responsible for the business running of what was left of Primal Scream.

Beattie's exit had been a serious blow, one that had totally altered the band's dynamic. From the start the band had been a mere fantasy inside the heads of Bobby and Jim - they pretty much agreed that even if it developed into a professional occupation they would be the only two members with authority. Now, with Jim gone, more emphasis was placed on guitarists Robert Young and Andrew Innes.

"Me, Robert and Andrew had a good thing going, I used to make Robert punk T-shirts and tapes when he was ten, that's why we've stuck together!" Bobby announced to the *NME* in '91, while three years later he said: "Rob's a great guitar player, but I don't think he thinks he's any good. He can't read music, I can't read music, but I think we've got good feeling, and it's that feeling that makes a group special to me." Robert and Andrew became central figures with Bobby and would share all writing credits from now onwards.

The core was settled. Bobby, Andrew and Robert put their hearts into Primal Scream and stayed united throughout the band's subsequent traumas. Outsiders would often be recruited for a particular task but the brotherhood mentality found in Gillespie, Innes and Young was now the quintessence of the group. Their considerable differences in personality gelled together to create a specific chemistry; an articulate and convincing whole that was every bit as genuine as that found in some of the greatest bands ever.

As the frontman, lyricist, mouthpiece to the press and remaining founder member, Bobby Gillespie for the most part handled his weighty responsibilities exceptionally well. Often criticised for his limited vocal range and his habit of talking at too great a length about things of too little importance, he always defended his group and insisted that they were in it to win it as one. His blatant exaggerations during interviews were never too difficult to notice, forming part of a character that saw a bubbly naivety mixed with a carefree attitude - he remains the most candid and down to earth rock star one could ever wish to meet.

Andrew Innes was an innovative rhythm guitarist, immersed in creating music of all different kinds. He would only escape his reserved nature in the studio or on stage, where he would often appear as excited as anyone. Beneath his quiet demeanour, Andrew remains as indulgent as anyone in the band, and is perhaps their most musical member; often lighting the spark when recording and providing that special something that can transform a song.

Robert Young, aka Throb, was over two years younger than Bobby, he had thick frizzy curls and a natural ability to pout - evidence of the fact that he was the most committed of the band to traditional rock. Learning both the bass and lead guitar via a mystery outfit named Black Easter, he'd transferred to Primal Scream in time for the debut single. With the exception of Bobby, Robert remains the longest serving member, and his almost complete lack of public utterances is proof of his focus on music rather than needless media fluff. He remains indisputably sly in the tight inner sanction of Primal Scream.

With drummer Gavin Skinner proving just a

stopgap, more musicians were needed to help them progress new ideas. Robert would hand the bass over to Henry Olsen while he took up the lead, and Phillip 'Toby' Tomanov was also recruited on drums when they were required to perform as a unit. The new rhythm section would not be full-time members.

Robert on the lead guitar was to have a profound effect. Ditching the Rickenbacker, Primal Scream returned with a live sound in the summer that had fattened with a more rasping style that immediately brought to mind The Ramones or The New York Dolls in their mid 70s splendour. They'd always played live to enjoy themselves, after all, performing was the very reason they first wanted to be in music. In order to make it pleasurable again the new material was raw and energetic. They also wrote some gentler numbers that were clearly designed to provide a change of pace to what was intended to be a well-balanced concert. They wanted to have a good time once more, feel more like rock stars and less like mice running round wheels, after all this was supposed to be the most fun career in the world.

Of the progress, Bobby explained: "In the old band, everything used to revolve around that pretty twelve string sound. Now Robert, who used to play bass, is playing guitar. So we've got two Les Pauls making this amazing raw sound. I know it's another cliche but this is the most settled line up we've ever had. You have to remember that the bands who inspired us to pick up guitars in the first place were The Sex Pistols and Public Image Limited. There's more space in the sound now. We're looser, funkier, and more fun."

In the mid 70s, disco music was a sensation in down-town New York and, although it eventually imploded following its adoption by the mainstream, it always flourished at underground clubs and illegal parties. Far from being the macho rock 'n' roll to which middle America flocked, it had begun as an almost exclusively urban, gay style of music. Moreover when Disc Jockeys started to experiment with new technology and edit together highlights of disco anthems it had a startling effect.

In Chicago by the early 1980s, DJs at a club called The Warehouse pioneered this technique to such an extent that when local clubbers went searching for the records they played they would just look for 'house' music and quickly it became clear to everyone what they meant. By the mid 1980s the DIY ethic of house had inspired legions of young black people in Chicago and soon, following experiments with accompanying bass tech-nology, the standard grooves were augmented by bleeping noises and traditional piano breaks. These sounds were before long named 'acid' house and they quickly crossed the Atlantic to the UK via the throbbing Mediterranean island of Ibiza - where on-the-ball holiday makers had noted how the beats seemed to mesh with a sphinx-like new chemical.

When British tourists returned it was to abandoned warehouses that they flocked for Britain's first illegal acid house parties - all hell would soon break loose.

By this time Primal Scream had gained an affectionate reputation. With the music press not quite the influence it would later become, it was still the music that mattered and perhaps because of this Alan McGee was becoming a personality in his own right. His enthusiasm saw him regarded as a fan, label boss, and two-bit rock star combined. When he attended a New Order aftershow party held by their label Factory at Manchester's Hacienda at Christmas '88, the after effects were consequently huge.

The Hacienda, the club Factory had opened some six years previously, was one of the first legitimate nightspots in the country that played this new form of music and it was already attracting media attention. By the time Alan visited the club it had found its feet as a dance temple as well as a live venue Primal Scream would occasionally play, and Alan felt the collective madness of a sea of hypnotised clubbers and knew he wanted more. He remembers: "I'd already done E, but that night there was pure ecstasy going round. I'd been going to clubs for ages but I'd never really got into acid house, I was just going round with Primal Scream trying to pick up women. I remember at seven in the morning being given a tablet and I was completely out of it." It was a defining occasion, as he first understood what this acid thing was all about and his discovery, of what was still mainly music intended for dancing to, had clear implications for his guitar dominated label.

Having separated from his wife, Alan promptly picked up and moved to Manchester to absorb as much of the hyped 'Madchester' scene as possible. Like Primal Scream, Manchester bands The Stone Roses and The Happy Mondays were turning a similar fascination with retro sounds into an attractive and increasingly danceable new cult. In later years it was reported that The Roses had started life as a brooding goth outfit until they began listening to Primal Scream, a claim that their bassist, Gary 'Mani' Mounfield, will these days confirm.

Before long, everyone everywhere it seemed was taken in by the heavenly marriage of the mysterious new love drug and acid house music. Along with records imported from American cities such as

Chicago, this devastating combination of pills and thrills had Britain's dancefloors packed with everyone from those hanging on from the punk explosion more than a decade before, to the football casual perhaps tired of the fighting.

Despite the lawlessness, those who took ecstasy appeared to love everyone, as there were hardly any reports of trouble at acid house parties at all. It was said to be a highly communal experience and for the next couple of years the thrill that could be had from indulging in this culture was omnipresent for Alan McGee; often sweeping aside the stresses of running a small record company. As long as the immediate bills were paid, nothing else seemed to matter, as very quickly he was living solely for the weekend.

At Alan's behest, and strictly as curious punters, Primal Scream began touring some of the hippest discothèques in the country. Along with Brighton's Zap Club, the venue where they found most comfort was Shoom, a converted gym in the London district of Southwark. Slowly they became attracted to the whole dance music scene and though not totally convinced of the music, they were impressed by the rather harmonious effect it was having on ecstasy users, as Bobby says: "All of the band were going out to clubs such as Shoom at the start of 1989. You couldn't help but be drawn into what was going on. If you want to talk about the rock 'n' roll lifestyle, look what was going on in the clubs. Compared to Primal Scream, you've got kids who do more drugs than us, and have more sex. Drugs are a massive thing in this country."

Primal Scream certainly didn't know it at the time, but those visits to nightclubs would be perhaps the most important thing they would ever do. While it had been pointed out to them during the past couple of years, it was only in amongst all the loose clothing of Britain's hip young clubbers that the band realised that leather trousers were highly unfashionable. Attitudes were beginning to change.

Once they submitted and began using ecstasy, they soon realised that acid house music and the drug that greased its wheels was alive with possibilities. Bobby soon claimed that in places where ecstasy was the fuel rather than alcohol, people were warm and nice; that it was more comforting to get wasted, which was just exactly what they loved to do. Before long they were having the time of their lives, though professionally those last months of the decade turned out to be their lowest-ever ebb.

The second album, released in September '89, was simply titled *Primal Scream*. It offered 'Ivy Ivy Ivy', 'You're Just Dead Skin To Me', 'She Power', 'You're Just Too Dark To Care', 'I'm Losing More Than I'll Ever Have', 'Gimme Gimme Teenage Head', 'Lone Star Girl', 'Kill The King', 'Sweet Pretty Thing' and 'Jesus Can't Save Me'. Bobby correctly commented: "I suppose the question everyone will want answering is 'where have we been all this time'? There's nothing particularly complicated to say. We've just been writing songs and trying to get a new sound. We aren't particularly prolific, but the sound we've got now we're really pleased with. We're going to blow people's heads off." He spoke too soon.

Loud screeching guitars and Bobby's sour vocals created a dense and often confusing listen. Put into the right frame of mind the new album was great fun; it contained distorted 'Beach Boys on acid' style surf rock and some fine ballads; the like of which had made bands like Led Zeppelin so appealing in previous eras; both heavy and light. Yet, if anyone found it appealing at the end of the 80s then it certainly wasn't the critics or the record buying public, as the album disappeared almost as soon as it arrived leaving everyone bitterly disappointed.

Bravely, they did what they could to defend its

appeal. It was a statement of their current standing. No longer were they neat popsters with innocent sounds and matching haircuts, but a dirtier, louder distortion of their former selves, intent on pushing their sound as far as it would go. It was glaringly obvious that they were playing only for themselves and hugely enjoying it. The fact that the album was recorded relatively quickly was proof of their desire to avoid the pitfalls of *Sonic Flower Groove*, which in comparison to its follow up sounded constrained and terribly unexciting. Their current influences were, as before, not difficult to identify.

Patti Smith had been an inspiration to legions of guitar-slashing bands who worked the 80s underground and Primal Scream were no exception, but this time around it was her husband Fred Smith's band MC5 with whom they were now generally compared. And they could hardly complain, especially since they'd cheekily acknowledged them by naming the imaginary producer for the album after their 'Sister Anne' song. In addition, recording their 'Ramblin' Rose' in a gloriously expansive way added credence to the old theory that imitation was the sincerest form of flattery, and with MC5, Primal Scream were hardly suggesting otherwise.

It had already been said enough times to become

meaningless that Primal Scream were plagiarists who illustrate their influences far too clearly but it's worth remembering that they were still in their mid-twenties and learning - just as The Byrds, MC5 and Iggy and The Stooges had seemed to inspire bands more than they sold records. But *Primal Scream* undoubtedly lacked a certain togetherness; it was a pretty untidy record, that not very successfully attempted to revel in juxtaposition rather than a continued theme, and also one that would appear to lose the band fans rather than gain them.

While it would be a mistake to say that they had no followers as they embarked on living out a fantasy of hard rocking excess, the appreciation society that had been founded after 'Velocity Girl' very noticeably stayed away. If there was a certain naive charm about the whimsical pop that smeared their first era, then it was unquestionably absent from the sleazy material that characterised much of the new record. A critical mauling could hardly have been unexpected in an era when, ironically, the jangly guitar sound of their recent past was suddenly flavour of the moment. By the looks of it, Primal Scream had peaked too early with their sonic flower power.

Now they could have stated, quite rightly, that they were at least two years ahead of their time with *Sonic*

Flower Groove, but instead they maintained a graceful distance from the debate and openly complimented the acts who'd rather stolen their thunder in 1989. Bobby happily explained that: "If we'd been a new band and released that album last year we'd have been huge. But that's the way pop music goes; you've got to be in the right place at the right time and I appreciate that because I love pop music."

Perhaps their eagerness to move away from the sweet sounds of their earliest records and react to the stresses of touring and Beattie leaving was a tad too hasty; when they re-emerged, they noticed the music climate celebrating loudly in their rear view mirror. Their current effort was sadly unloved by the majority and its cold dismissal plainly illustrated the importance of timing in pop. The lifespan of *Primal Scream* was staggeringly brief and its impact was minimal.

Its opening song and lead single 'Ivy Ivy Ivy' sounded like punk before it reached Britain, with the listener at once taken by an arresting drum smack and aggressive guitar that was far more Jesus And Mary Chain on speed than The Byrds on acid. They sounded like a garage band having fun with Andrew, after his fairly limited input on the last album, releasing wave after wave of crunching string work via an assortment of distortion effects. As one reviewer wrote, it spun around chewing bubble gum for three minutes, and by the time it ended, you weren't quite sure if they were the best or worst band in the world.

The first song was a yardstick for half the record, as 'She Power', 'Gimme Gimme Teenage Head', 'Lone Star Girl' and 'Sweet Pretty Thing' all followed with similar formulae, while an obvious immaturity stalked the lyrics that were backed up here and there by some Beach Boys-esque harmonies. It added a comedic element to the songs that bordered on the well-worn sentiment of kitsch sing-a-longs. The vocals were somewhat buried in the mix but the lyrics could still be understood; they were of the boy girl variety that gave away little more than the dumb song titles.

But it wasn't all hip thrusting, hand-clapping glam overkill, as the second number revealed that this was a very different band to the one that had cut *Sonic Flower Groove*. 'You're Just Dead Skin To Me' featured a propelling piano, harmonica and a nicely balanced combination of deft electric guitar and ugly feedback. It was an uneasy listen, full of pain and despair, that was very much uncharted territory for Primal Scream and if nothing else proved their willingness to experiment. 'You're Just Too Dark To Care', 'Kill The King' and 'Jesus Can't Save Me' followed suit and the attraction of 'I'm Losing More Than I'll Ever Have' at the time looked to be no more than that of another rather pretentious but touching ballad.

Alan sent the band out on the road to build up confidence as critical perception was starting to prove more powerful than reality, while Bobby defiantly proved that his PR skills were well and truly intact. "The live shows are going to blow people away," he told the press, "we've got the right attitude, a real arrogance but at the same time we want to give people a really good time. Those Les Pauls are going to be screaming!" After an uncertain start, when they were regarded in some quarters as Judas characters for betraying their jangly origins, the shows were in truth just as Bobby warned, he proved sharp and incisive; and he was right about the guitars.

Touring for months on end that autumn, Primal Scream often visited clubs in places that were hardly large population centres. In the likes of Bolton, Reading, Bristol and Dudley, night after night they turned in a stormer, relaxing in comfort away from cynical reviewers. On stage Bobby would wail into his microphone as if it were his best friend while Andrew and Robert tore into their instruments as if they were about to die in a plane crash. It didn't matter if they weren't as good as their idols, just as long as they believed they were, as they didn't lose money and no-one could have been under any serious illusions of changing the world. If only for entertainment's sake then a curious, poverty-stricken student rock fan in a half-empty club could ask for no more.

That a live recording was never considered was unfortunate because Primal Scream didn't reach as many people as they would have liked with this shameless rock 'n' roll show. The new songs were designed to be performed live and just as well as the recorded versions simply didn't do the new material justice. The songs, which always promised much, now bloomed before live audiences underlining their problems in the studio where their two albums to date had so far seen them too cautious and too casual, which had resulted in their raw material remaining no more than unfulfilled potential.

The flip side, however, was that when inspiration struck at an unlikely moment, without concern for preconceived continuity, the creative juices flowed and provided them with some of their finest work. 'It Happens', for example, was superior to 'All Fall Down', and 'Velocity Girl', of course, bedazzled in comparison to 'Crystal Crescent'. Perhaps they strained under the pressure of trying to deliver an LP that appealed to everyone, but the experiments and songs that didn't quite fit plan A saw Primal Scream flourish into something akin to Bobby's initial idea of the band. When it mattered they just needed to compose themselves and relax, and that time would come; sooner or later it was bound to.

While playing like The New York Dolls, Primal Scream were socialising on tour like overgrown students suddenly liberated from the restraints of family life. Their introduction to ecstasy at the height of their flirtation with greasy biker punk resulted in a flood feeling of both release and novelty. They were certain of their priorities but their curiosity, particularly post show, saw them further channel their energies to community clubbing and almost dancing. Much as the concerts were going well, they actually did little more than keep the faith with the band, who were already pondering their next move. The cool vibe of seaside Brighton made Glasgow seem like a forgotten wasteland and they soon gathered that they too could be part of this exciting new world from which they were currently cast adrift. A lingering air of optimism loomed as they began absorbing new music and meeting new people with great enthusiasm. They demonstrated their new found vigour by playing louder and faster.

Banging their heads in front of small and indifferent

audiences in Europe that winter, their minds were so far from the album that it was decided to cancel the remainder of the trip and get back to swinging Britain as soon as possible. The last thing Primal Scream could ever be accused of was discipline but what apparently happened on that fateful outing may well stand as their *tour de force* of carelessness. Be it for reasons of poor communication or naivety, not everyone learned of the dates being scrapped and as a result crew and equipment arrived in eastern Europe without the band who had either flown home or lost themselves in various states of relaxation. Bobby claimed, maybe only half jokingly, that he woke up once and didn't know what country he was in. They'd had enough and the tour just collapsed. It sounded irresponsible, yet amusing.

Sadly though, nothing could disguise the fact that *Primal Scream* had failed to make any impact commercially and with the press seemingly obsessed with flare-wearing Manchester bands, an uncertain future loomed. The doubtful hardly diminished when they learned that Shoom DJ Andy Weatherall, who had noticed them about in Brighton had, as invited, proactively remixed one of their songs. Word was that the outcome was intended to be dance music.

Strange.

As a young punk in Windsor Andrew Weatherall covered himself in tattoos and grew his hair. Something of a juvenile delinquent at the time, he admits to being in the right place at the right time.

By the late 80s, following spells doing a number of menial jobs including bricklaying, Andy had met Terry Farley, who shared his interest in music, fashion and football. The two of them started an avant-garde fanzine called *Boy's Own* that was soon considered a leading voice by regulars at Shoom, whose smart clientele made up a considerable part of its readership.

Moving to London in 1988 Andy found himself living in the same Battersea council flat as Alex Paterson, who would soon launch The Orb, and his mate Youth, formerly of Killing Joke. Friends of Youth and Paterson, Weatherall and Farley were regular spinners at Shoom, and through his fanzine work Andy landed a freelance position with the *NME*. The paper had assigned him to review the Primal Scream concert at the Exeter Arts Centre on 21 September. Under the pseudonym 'Audrey Witherspoon', his report wasn't especially complimentary.

"I reviewed the gig at Exeter," says Andy, "I'd seen them about at clubs but when I met them the first words Bobby Gillespie said to me were: 'Is that a perm or is your hair really that curly?' They're a tight-knit bunch and the fact that the hair was a bit Marc Bolan-esque broke the ice. It was a fun night, we all went on to a discotheque and ran out because a fight started when the DJ played 'Lip Up Fatty' by Bad Manners..."

There is much debate over who first suggested Andy remixing Primal Scream; but whether it was recently converted raver Alan McGee, the innovative Primal Scream member Andrew Innes, or Creation's long-serving publicist Jeff Barrett, one thing was for certain: not everyone was happy with the prospect of a rock band making dance music. It was, not unreasonably, seen as a contradiction to their image, an unforgivable act of large scale treason. Those who clung to that belief nowadays prefer to remain nameless.

"We knew that Andy Weatherall liked our group and that was at a time when very few people liked what we did," says Bobby, "and we loved what he played as a DJ, and we knew that he was into really good music and that he was open-minded. Also, the fact that he'd never been in a studio before was a plus. It was pretty experimental in that sense..."

The guinea pig track was 'I'm Losing More Than I'll Ever Have', the fifth number on the album and arguably their finest song to date. Even taking into account Gillespie's showy, gut wrenching and unoriginal lyric, it was undoubtedly *Primal Scream*'s one truly masterful song and for remix potential it was as appropriate as any. Weatherall loved its slow burning rhythms and skyscraping climax. Perhaps the result of his knob twiddling would grace the B side of a future single, but surely no more; any more exposure would betray everything that Primal Scream appeared to stand for. Still, he took up the challenge and his enthusiasm went a very long way indeed.

Taking a drum loop from a recording of Edie Brickell's sassy hit 'What I Am' which cut a Soul II Soul like hypnotic groove, removing all lyrics and adding funky piano from Martin Duffy, a friend who'd played on the album - Andy shaped not just the much needed watershed in Primal Scream's career but also, as far as British indie music was concerned, one of the land-mark songs of the following decade.

screamadelica

Weatherall's remix of 'I'm Losing More Than I'll Ever Have' would feature dialogue from Roger Corman's cult film *The Wild Angels*, spoken by actor Peter Fonda. When seeking permission to use them, Creation sent an employee to Peter's sister Jane to ask her to contact him and check if it was okay. Thankfully it was, while Roger only asked for one pence from every copy sold. Such was the perceived importance of the dialogue to the new record that, on the all clear, the collective sigh of relief breathed by the band in Brighton could be heard back in Glasgow. Testing the water, and perhaps trying to spark some belated life into the album, in the final weeks of the year 'I'm Losing More Than I'll Ever Have' was pushed out on limited release to club DJs who Creation knew would be more interested in the new remix now titled 'Loaded', named after the dialogue, on the B side.

Weatherall first played the seven minute 'Loaded' at a London club called Subterania and that night at least, it seemed to perfectly capture the mood of the clubbers who were, safe to say, fairly typical of those who understood acid house. Back from Europe in one piece,

Bobby remembers: "Andy was playing it in clubs, and he was phoning us up saying 'everyone's going nuts to this record'. And we thought, 'hey, we might have a hit here!'"

If its immediate tempo wasn't so gloriously sluggish, 'Loaded' might be described as conventional rave, being built around the smouldering outro from 'I'm Losing More...' and an infectious drum loop. But without lyrics or even a chorus, the inclusion of sunken guitar, gospel vocals, seductive piano and muted bagpipe samples created something entirely new. In the hundreds of words that have since been written about the record, for the most part the initial appeal was always the novelty; there had quite literally never been anything like it, and certainly not from a band like Primal Scream but by early 1990 that didn't seem to matter.

The country was going through a huge change as mass dancing and drug-taking propelled unlikely guitar bands onto the airwaves of the nation's most listened to radio station. Following the full explosion of the Madchester boom across the nation's music press finally, and very long last, BBC Radio One simply had no option but to play the breezy, exciting new music from bands providing a much needed breath of fresh air. Suddenly the station was pumping out the chiming guitars and spellbinding beats of The Stone Roses and The Happy Mondays in a way that would have been impossible two years before. The floodgates were open; it was out with the old and in with the new as the underground celebrated a comprehensive victory.

It was precisely the right time then for Primal Scream to unleash their own attempt at combining rock and dance. Advance copies of 'Loaded' had been causing a major buzz on Britain's dancefloors and at well connected radio stations but while feedback was encouraging, it was no guarantee of the track becoming a bona fide hit. After literally thousands of enquires, the Primal Scream/Andy Weatherall collaboration was commercially released with high hopes in February and quickly grew into the most successful single Creation had ever released.

At last critics fell over themselves to sing the praises of a Primal Scream song. For so long a notorious gang of retro outsiders, they were now dragging rock music into the 90s with a sensational new sound. They at last penetrated the country's official chart when 'Loaded' reached number sixteen, supported by a debut appearance on celebrated television show *Top Of The Pops*. Appearing far too aloof to consider themselves fortunate to be there and standing next to the usual chart fodder, Primal Scream swayed and stumbled through a mime of an edited cut, leaving observers wondering just how they found what was undoubtedly the highest point of their career so far.

"The first time we played *TOTP*, we did 'Loaded'," Bobby explained over twelve years later, "but they had to use the rehearsal take because we were too, well, loaded to perform." Looking at the broadcast it is difficult to tell if the band were fully taking in the spirit of the whole occasion but going on the programme must have felt like a triumph for such ardent lovers of pop culture. They were now a group with a hit; it suddenly all made sense. It had taken six long years but Primal Scream had finally arrived. The domestic success led to Creation quickly arranging for their current work to be distributed by Warner Brothers' Sire subsidiary in America where the single would also chart in several dance arenas.

Such was the current mood that live dates were quickly arranged in Europe and Asia for the first time. Only a few months previously Primal Scream's set was from a traditional voice, guitar, bass and drums outfit. It was a no-frills rock show, with no sign of the dance element that had now crept into their thinking. Performed every night in a capably traditional way, 'Loaded' was always the evening's highlight, enjoyed by all and was quickly adopted as a genuine anthem by hoards of teenagers fascinated by this slice of British culture.

In Japan, they developed a fanatical following, proven by one act of devotion in particular - as impressive as any homage to any boy band. Upon learning of Bobby's unsuccessful search for the soundtrack to The Monkees' film *Head*, a dedicated group of fans searched Tokyo, found a pristine copy of the record and duly presented it to the singer at one of the shows. Bobby was thrilled at the gesture, leaving him in good spirits before he underwent a minor operation to remove surplus ear wax that had been causing him discomfort.

Perhaps inevitably, on the back of the two hundred thousand-selling 'Loaded', many of Primal Scream's peers immediately launched scathing attacks on the band claiming that they'd betrayed their guitar roots and were taking too much credit for what had mostly been Weatherall's work. Since they always fully credited Andy, who was only really rearranging sounds they'd written and performed, the accusations were quickly brushed aside. Yet because of Primal Scream, Weatherall had turned from unknown disc jockey to a creative, skilled professional regularly referred to as a mastermind by the adoring press. Something was happening; Primal Scream and their rapidly growing entourage were apparently leading a new movement called 'indie dance'. How long it would last remained to be seen. For now though, good times were most definitely to be had.

The moment had finally arrived when they grasped that they; the uncool band from Glasgow could be as creative, genre ignorant, and downright audacious as any of their musical influences. The gamble with the remix had paid off beyond their wildest dreams; it was a triumph comparable to any U-turn down the years and, no doubt enviously observing how for almost a year now The Happy Mondays had been polishing the dancefloor, a sharp Primal Scream were perhaps the first act to consciously react and acknowledge the effect in those heaving student discos. Of course there would be those who opposed; it might have been a couple of years before their *C86* fans could have the old sound back as the Scream team had entered an unimaginable period of high fashion.

As 'Loaded' spilled everywhere from student parties to commercial radio stations it shouldn't be forgotten that it had all been a huge experiment. Never could Primal Scream have expected it to be acclaimed as the single of the year but when it was it left them with a huge dilemma: what to do next? Having successfully embraced dance culture once, the fuse was lit and there was now seemingly no limit to just how far they could go. The obvious decision was made to switch wholesale and radically reinvent themselves into a dance orientated groove machine.

While the signs had been there it can't have been a simple decision since as recently as the interview rounds for *Primal Scream* Bobby had expressed a complete disinterest in such an idea; he'd told the *NME*: "We're not that stupid. We couldn't do it if we tried. When white people make dance records they just turn the snare up." At the time of those comments, it's likely that Gillespie was just too proud to admit that his beloved rock 'n' roll was no longer at the centre of the musical universe. Seeing what ecstasy and acid house had done for people on the dancefloor had scorched the minds of Primal Scream and, as a rock act, they knew they were in danger of being left behind. They've always aspired to be the best band they can be and now the extraordinary success of 'Loaded' saw them not only make up the ground, but surge well into the lead in the supposed race for the first genuine post acid house record. They went to work.

Periodically at London's Jam Studios in Finsbury Park and their own more modest set-up in the Isle Of

Dogs they partied, wrote and recorded new songs that they realised very early on were quite unlike anything they'd done before. Samples, tape loops and dub sounds were suddenly at the forefront of ideas keeping writing fresh and exciting. The change in the band became almost as visual as it was audible. Bobby's floppy shoulder length hair had been replaced by a smart fringe while the leathers also made way for bright colours of silk, trainers and loose denim. Also, far from being the tight brooding gang of recent years they were now loved-up and welcoming everyone's influence and input especially to the mixing, a production stage that now assumed huge significance.

Terry Farley was brought in to assist on a new song they had called 'Come Together'. Bobby sang to the accompaniment of neat slide guitar lines yet on Weatherall's more ambient mix, a ten-minute marathon featuring the preaching civil rights campaigner Jesse Jackson, he was again completely absent but nevertheless the hottest interviewee in town.

Of 'Come Together' he said: "I think the Weatherall side is really inflammatory. It's beautiful but at the same time it's really militant and tough. Both sides of that record are brilliant. People are going to have to try hard to beat that and I hope someone does. In a way, we've thrown the gauntlet down. We've done 'Come Together' and if I was in another band I'd think: 'They're brilliant records, I'm going to go beyond that'."

To an extent he was right, as indie kids far and wide were waking to up the possibilities of dance, while with either version of 'Come Together' they had again come up with what was pretty much the most innovate single of the year. Both mixes had the critics foaming, inventing phrases such as 'gospel dance anthem'. The video that accompanied the Farley mix appeared the most enjoyable performance they would ever give. The psychedelic lights, balloons and sultry dancing were much the first indicators of their visual transformation, and helped by Bobby's first *NME* cover story 'Come Together' reached number twenty-six.

In 1990 a top thirty placing was considered a crowning achievement by the still indisputably independent labels. If a song was good enough, it was now almost guaranteed to sell well, helped perhaps by the added publicity offered by the 24-hour cable music channels. Ultimately though, without a hope of competing with the majors that could afford to package their acts for the masses, the launch point for the promotion of new music was always the same; the ever more influential and now fully revitalised music papers. Looking back, Madchester and acid house had so much to answer for.

Primal Scream were fortunate, as to thousands of weekenders who indeed loved to get loaded, they were a new act that existed only on the disc jockey's turntables and not the concert stages of Britain's rock clubs. The papers were slowly coming to realise that there was a dance culture with a following sizeable enough that, if catered for, could virtually guarantee an increase in readership. The stadium acts that had dominated the press throughout the previous decade had overreached themselves, leaving editors stuck for something topical to report; they felt that many readers were moving on to music that wasn't being covered by their writers and, once they realised this, Primal Scream and a select handful of others managed to move into the empty space.

Without wishing to state the obvious; good music has never been just about the top ten. Many artists have been commended for their refusal to play the promotional game, as it has long been considered a crime that compromises musical integrity; a theory very much endorsed by Andrew Innes and Robert Young. Now Primal Scream did occasionally play the game; they made videos and mimed on television programmes but their use of the print media was by far the biggest reason that their fan base began to grow.

Bobby would always find time for writers who'd finally acknowledged that his band could now help sell ever more copies of their journals. He seemed to enjoy gloating on the back of the recent successes and in some cases invited certain journalists to eat humble pie. Other scribes rightly pointed out that a couple of innovative singles didn't make them a truly great band and that future music would now be under intense scrutiny. Major grades were now expected, a fact Bobby privately acknowledged.

In spite of the heights he and his house band had scaled, Alan sensed that Rough Trade's distribution was struggling from a combination of self-inflicted wounds and plain bad luck. Now that Creation was enjoying critical and chart success, Alan looked for more exposure and blamelessly defected from the crumbling empire, opting instead for Pinnacle, Rough Trade's main rivals in the independent sector. Not surpisingly Rough Trade collapsed completely within months, while Pinnacle competently distributed Creation in its final era as a strutting independent. Now that Creation's cornerstone band was in the top thirty there was ample evidence to believe that the move was for the best.

The recording party was in full swing. The sessions were so ill-disciplined that it was commonplace for band members to stagger into the studio after a marathon session in a nightspot and experiment with whatever instrument happened to be to hand. While recording came together quite slowly, an impulsiveness was captured from the energy and mellowness of their clubbing experiences. Tim Tooher, a sometime Creation Artist and Repertoire man, wrote a passionate article that appeared in *Mojo* a couple of years later. When they were recording the new material he joyously revealed that: "Every night Bob would come back to my flat. We'd spend hours together; reading and listening to records and in that time I watched their album grow. Bob would play 'The Most Beautiful Girl' by Charlie Rich and 'I'm Stone In Love With You' by The Stylistics and as the sun shone into the room, the records seemed to carry the sound of the new day."

The feeling was of liberation, as the limitations of their voice, guitar, bass and drums conventions were cast aside; thanks to them finally discovering musical restraint. Bobby told MTV of their new found dash to recording: "We just started trying different things and we built our own little studio where we could experiment and learn as well with a lot of different instruments, whereas before what we had was like bass, two guitars, vocals and drums - so we were kind of limited by that." While he, Andrew and Robert remained central, Henry Olsen, Toby Tomanov, Andy Weatherall and his engineer Hugo Nicholson all offered their hands, providing an input that helped emphasise not what you did play, but what you didn't.

As a result Bobby, for example, was often happy to sit it out when it was felt that vocals wouldn't be necessary and Andrew was likewise encouraged to move away from the guitar. Of the additions to the team, arguably the most hedonistic of them all was classically trained pianist Martin Duffy, who they had first come in contact with towards the end of the 80s when he was barely out of his teens and playing with Felt, a little known but acclaimed Creation outfit from his native Birmingham. Appreciating the contribution Martin had made to the second album and acknowledging the importance of piano to their breakthrough sound, Primal Scream permanently recruited him from the ashes of Felt towards the end of 1990.

Into the new year former PiL bassist Jah Wobble played on a mix of the next single, the appropriately titled 'Higher Than The Sun'. This time the mood was spacious; blues-orientated with hints of jazz.

If 'Loaded' and 'Come Together' had been composed to soundtrack a euphoric night on the dancefloor, then 'Higher Than The Sun' was a completely different entity. Mixed by The Orb, it seemed to be above anything they'd done before; with its cold ambience and plodding cyber beat, it was perhaps the most suitable music yet for Bobby's voice and was equally effective in concert or on record. Speaking to *Rage*, the singer beamed: "It's as good as anything I've ever heard; as good as T Rex, The Temptations, or The Rolling Stones. We've actually made a classic record. It's a record that people will be able to listen to in forty years time and it's still going to be as relevant then as it is now."

A fourth single (the release of which was held until August) entitled 'Don't Fight It, Feel It', saw them experiment further by having radiant Manchester diva Denise Johnson take over the vocals. Denise was singing with Hypnotone, a not wholly successful Creation act when Andrew first noticed her. Denise's beaming presence would grace Primal Scream for the next four years, often lifting spirits during some of the difficult times ahead. In 1991 'Don't Fight It, Feel It' was the most radical departure yet from the jangly guitar pop that had characterised the band previously and was probably the final straw for many of their early fans. Equally radically, the shimmering house track featured the new recruits in starring roles.

"We play the keyboards and guitars, though the guitars don't sound like guitars because they've been treated", Bobby explained at the time and, of Denise's involvement he went on: "It's like when Lou Reed got Nico to sing because he thought she could do a better job. I don't have an ego about it." With Weatherall again taking care of production, the Scream family was growing exponentially as if something truly special was beginning to take shape.

The subsequent live dates, many would agree, captured Primal Scream at the absolute height of their cult appeal. Despite the complete turn around in musical style, ticket sales were healthy as word soon spread about the show being a new kind of event. Word proved affirmative. It was like New Year's Eve every night.

In non-traditional venues, The Orb would open the show, warming up the considerably more colourful audience than in previous years for Primal Scream's first nationwide tour since their commercial breakthrough. On vocals there was Bobby Gillespie and Denise Johnson, on guitars Andrew Innes and Robert Young, on keys Martin Duffy, on bass Henry

Olsen, on drums Toby Tomanov and taking care of sample duties was Hugo Nicholson. When they all took to the stage they would play a fashionably short set. Including the four singles, songs performed included brand new numbers like 'Movin' On Up' and 'Damaged', while 'I'm Losing More Than I'll Ever Have' was aired along with covers like the 13th Floor Elevators' 'Slip Inside This House' and John Lennon's 'Cold Turkey'.

Recreating the songs with their new synths and faithful guitars resulted in a fascinating mixture of sounds that were well supported by the visuals. Bobby would spin across the stage, hopping and clapping with complete abandon, like some exaggerated young clubber in-between slurring lyrics about love, having a good time and heartbreak. Either side of him, Robert and Andrew reassured older fans by attacking their six-strings behind a tightly curled wall of rock star hair. The pair existed, primarily, in a rock 'n' roll band and, watching them on stage with their boots cocked high on the monitors and loose shirts flapping wildly, it was clear that however much the technology benefited them it was never going to tear them from their first love.

"We've always been a rock 'n' roll band," Robert told *Select* in 1993, "although we sometimes use the available technology, if you see us live, it's a rock 'n' roll guitar band, it's always been one and it always will be." After the band Andy Weatherall went behind the decks and took the audience well into the early hours with his own ever more distinctive style of DJing. It was a club night with a rock 'n' roll show in-between.

It was a sign of just how much the preconceptions of dance culture had changed. Not three years previously Primal Scream wouldn't have considered even attending an event where the attraction was someone merely playing records; back then that sort of thing was seen as the enemy - a threat to their livelihood. But their post-ecstasy emotions compelled them to welcome ravers, as well as rockers, to their shows and what's even more surprising is that there wasn't a drop of pride involved. Bobby in particular insisted that it wasn't just about Primal Scream and that The Orb and Weatherall should be given equal billing.

"It's a whole night," he said, "it's not like the normal rock thing where they've got one or two support bands and then the main act comes on. With us everything's as important as everything else. The Orb [Alex Paterson] he plays first and he gets the audience really kickin', right, and then we come on and we give it to them, the rock 'n' roll thing, right, and then we come off and Andy gives it to them with the records that he plays, so that people all night are just on a constant high. It's a totally different atmosphere, it's wonderful."

As the circus gathered momentum, their reputation for hedonism was such that promoters worried about the band's treatment of venues and in true rock star fashion hotel rooms were suddenly getting trashed with alarming frequency. Reminiscing of the immaturity of it all, Bobby explained several times how they just couldn't resist the temptations that were laid before them. "At the time it was great," he remembers, "but that kind of fame is always a bit destabilising. We were just being ourselves but we were in the thick of it too. Everybody wants to hang out with you - the parties were mad anyway, but they were getting madder. Even by our standards, we were right out there."

Seeing the band that summer was an experience that everyone wanted; the hangers-on, the journalists, the friends of friends, the fans, they all wanted a piece of this revolutionary band who performed songs worthy of Kraftwerk in a manner more reminiscent of The Rolling Stones. They took a sledgehammer to convention and those lucky enough to see them in action must have been curious enough to wonder what was going on behind the scenes. The rumour was that the backstage enclosure was a mass orgy of certain activities that were highly addictive and not all of them were legal.

Following them around with a major piece of video recording equipment was Douglas Hart, former bassist in The Jesus And Mary Chain. Unfortunately, for reasons that have never been made clear, his proposed fly-on-the-wall style rockumentary was never shown to the general public, though some of his footage was cut to the soundtrack of 'Slip Inside This House' for release with no fewer than nine other promos on a longform video that would follow the forthcoming album.

Since the surprise success of 'Loaded', Primal Scream had had a further three magnificent singles and an acclaimed tour that should have confirmed that they were finally the real thing. A year and a half since the breakthrough had been time enough for doubts to be raised about their work rate, while the following singles, as brilliant as they were, still couldn't fully silence the cynical press.

It seems they didn't compromise their work ethic in any case. "The main thing is making a great record and having a good time doing it," Bobby explained to *NME* journo James Brown, "if that wasn't the case, there'd have been quick follow-ups to both 'Loaded' and 'Come Together' when they were in the charts. I love it when a band can produce four good singles in as many months but we can't do that, we work in our own time scale." Nevertheless, since the releases after 'Loaded' had progressively sold less, Alan was worried that the bubble was beginning to burst. In fact, he was depending on the new Primal Scream album to lift spirits and his label's entire financial status.

Thankfully, as their song goes, and despite some apparent internal doubt, everything really did come together, with Bobby humbly speaking of the new LP: "Just so long as it moves people, makes them feel good. It's like if these songs can bring some joy to people then it's alright." For once, when modesty was evident from Gillespie, he would have looked much better with his usual arrogance, as the album turned out better than he could have possibly imagined.

For every musical vogue there's always at least one album that typifies it perfectly, one that's acclaimed, popular, and will be forever fashionable. *Screamadelica* is one of those albums. The climate that gave birth to Primal Scream's whimsically titled new long player was the acid house fall out, when young people would confidently go out, take ecstasy, dance to electronic music, fall in love and then go home and play classic, mellow pop to soothe their emotions. As unlikely as it may have seemed during the heyday of acid house, with their third album Primal Scream created the perfect soundtrack to the heady nights it spawned.

The first thing you especially noticed was the packaging; designer Paul Cannell's glaring saucer-eyed sunshine looked like the result of an afternoon's work in kindergarten. It was liberating (fresh from the usual rock star pose and elaborate font) grabbing the attention instantly. It was incandescent with optimism and youthful energy; the pure red, yellow and blue complemented each other, adding much to the freehand shapes and made their layered structure quite sensational in appearance. The logo soon appeared on posters, T-shirts and provided a huge backdrop for live performances later in the year. It was already the best record sleeve of the year but what about the music it was representing?

Released in September '91, *Screamadelica* was the result of nearly two years of non-stop partying. Former Rolling Stones producer Jimmy Miller had worked on 'Movin' On Up' and 'Damaged' - two styles of the classic rock track - whilst Hugo Nicholson helped Weatherall produce almost every other song. The results were spectacular. With repeated playing

Screamadelica created an absolutely thrilling new world of freedom, innovation and inspiration. It was as if Primal Scream had captured the resulting high from all the hip substances floating around in a package that was both long lasting and highly accessible.

The perfect time capsule, it offered: 'Movin' On Up', 'Slip Inside This House', 'Don't Fight It, Feel It', 'Higher Than The Sun', 'Inner Flight', 'Come Together', 'Loaded', 'Damaged', 'I'm Comin' Down', 'Higher Than The Sun (a dub symphony in two parts)' and 'Shine Like Stars'.

"This is the first LP where we're totally happy with everything on it; our songwriting is better than it's ever been and the great thing about it is, it's the first time we've used real producers who've helped us focus our ideas, people like Andy, Hugo, Jimmy Miller and The Orb," Bobby explained.

While conscious of the fact that the record was a considerable risk, as it would almost certainly alienate the bulk of their followers who could, not unreasonably, claim that they'd sold out to dance fashion, the undeniable truth was that Primal Scream had delivered the finest album of their career and although it may have taken a while, everyone from the kid on the street to the elitist rock critic couldn't deny the striking originality on offer.

That the songs fitted together so well was a total coincidence. 'Loaded' was the centrepiece, which had already been released, as had 'Come Together', 'Higher Than The Sun' and 'Don't Fight It, Feel It', while the cover of 'Slip Inside This House' had the year before appeared on Sire's tribute LP to its composer Roky Erikson. 'Movin' On Up' and 'Damaged' were admittedly as good as anything they had recorded but in comparison, the remaining numbers appeared to an unconvinced few as nothing more than fillers that showcased the talent and vision of Andy Weatherall. Primal Scream indeed actually only had little more than half an LP complete; that's not to say that *Screamadelica* was a forced compilation but it seemed too good to be true; it was sensational, wonderful, glorious; it contained the most revolutionary new music in years.

Reflecting the mood of the times in glorious technicolour, the album was hailed as a masterpiece by virtually every reviewer: "*Screamadelica* is one of this era's most beautiful far-reaching pieces of musical adventure, sustained by club culture and brain-wacky chemicals... it will be recognised as a benchmark" raved the *NME*. "A small step onto the dancefloor for Bobby and co, but a giant leap for you and me. Ten-out-of-ten," confirmed *Vox*. "Standard rock etiquette is replaced by that of the dancefloor to thrilling effect," said *Q. Melody Maker* meanwhile claimed that: "Primal Scream have made a record as good as any of the greats they so obviously rejoice in. *Screamadelica* is truly, literally wonderful." *Select* concluded that it was "a listening experience of wild, vivid imagination" before awarding five-out-of-five and, later, the album of the year honour.

Even by 1996, *Select* went so far as to declare it as the very best album of the decade so far. Ten years after its release, *Q,* the world's biggest selling music monthly, asked its readers to vote for the fifty greatest albums since its launch in 1986 and while the poll was topped by Radiohead's 1997 LP *OK Computer*, *Screamadelica* came in second, ahead of landmark albums by the likes of Nirvana, R.E.M. and U2. Even estranged founder member Jim Beattie, then treading the boards with Spirea X, was moved to comment: "I think there's a lot of good noises on it. Primal Scream did something different. If I saw Bobby I'd have a pint with him."

In 1991 then, far from being the laughing stock of just two years before, Primal Scream could now do no wrong. They'd released an LP that was shredding everything in sight; one that reviewers simply could not praise highly enough and one that, significantly, helped stubborn indie kids understand the grand possibilities of rock and dance music mixed together. Not since New Order's grouping of gloomy basslines and computerised beats a decade earlier had music landed with such force, sounding so of its time, ahead of its time and quite probably timeless all at once. Bobby Gillespie was walking it like he'd been talking it for years and there was no major gloating, but rather encouragement to all to enjoy music that came from his band but now belonged to the world.

Yet on its first airing it couldn't be denied that overall the album was something of a let down. But for 'Movin' On Up' and maybe 'Damaged', there was little resemblance to the band's previous work. Two years into the 90s though, *Screamadelica* was often referred to as 'indie's first dance rock record' and it quickly had boys with guitars everywhere clambering for the remixers. Andy Weatherall's telephone barely stopped ringing, as he'd done such a good job that it virtually secured his future. His subsequent career would expand as The Sabres Of Paradise, Two Lone Swordsmen and further remix work with the likes of Bjork, Stereo MCs and New Order. The concept of the superstar remixing DJ was rapidly gathering pace and with *Screamadelica* as a reference, Weatherall's immortality was nigh on assured. He would be awarded the sobriquet 'Techno's Phil Spector.'

Back on the road in Japan the band were treated like royalty and at home in Glasgow, during the second British circuit of the year in much bigger venues, *Q* writer Miranda Sawyer finally got the infamous interview that many suspected was in Bobby somewhere but had yet to come out - as he casually told the journalist: "if you look at our band and you look at the drug usage involved, it's not just as simple as ecstasy. It's basically everything you can think of. How could I put it? A lot of what we do is quite strung out and quite... heroin-y." Miranda insisted that no exaggeration was employed when penning the article, leaving the best hope to be that Bobby was by now amusing himself with his answers, for what literally could have been interview number one hundred and something. As with the infamous Mary Chain riot story, the publicity could only add to the record's success.

Sales of *Screamadelica* were by far the strongest of Primal Scream's career as the album was glued to the top ten, a situation that should have helped Creation towards full time security. Of their other releases, those by Teenage Fanclub and My Bloody Valentine were also massive creative successes, giving Alan some real muscle when selling rights on to international labels and distributors. For the first time in its history the company could look to a future that seemed almost secure. But only almost.

Unfortunately, My Bloody Valentine's spiralling LP *Loveless* had gone over budget by at least four hundred percent and the fact that it was critically acclaimed upon its eventual release was only a vindication of sorts for Alan who realised that his relaxed yet passionate attitude simply could not continue. MBV were dumped, leaving Creation chronically in debt and, though the brilliant records were coming thicker and faster than ever, their required production funds just weren't there. Running a small record company had already by far exceeded McGee's ambitions but in the wake of *Loveless*, the financial practicalities of doing so were denying him his rightful profit. It was make or break time for Creation as its founder began to look for ways towards a more secure future. Primal Scream meanwhile, were soaring.

The New Ardent Studios were opened in Memphis, Tennessee in 1971. Aside from the numerous classic records that had been cut there, perhaps the greatest cult band of their era, Big Star, had virtually formed there whilst working as a technical crew at the facilities not long after they opened. Primal Scream were huge fans of Big Star and also of their producer, celebrated pianist Jim Dickinson. Famed for his work with everyone from The Rolling Stones to Ry Cooder, Dickinson was contacted by Bobby in November as Primal Scream were in town to shoot a video and sample the delights of Ardent for themselves. Though a musical collaboration was not specifically discussed, the meeting with the pianist was a marker for Bobby as, like an excited tourist, he went to great lengths to explain his appreciation of Jim's work, who in turn was taken by Gillespie's knowledge.

While back in Britain the album had everyone spinning on the dancefloor, thousands of miles across the Atlantic the authors of that important domestic statement took to another agenda completely. Years later, Bobby claimed that with *Screamadelica* they simply wanted to make a great rock 'n' roll album and again that as a band, they loved to get wasted. Drugs and music had gone together since day one and with the inspiration having come from ecstasy, very much a new kid on the block, Primal Scream were quite unwittingly being hailed as leaders of the E movement. Thus if "when in Rome do as the Romans do", then when in Memphis, you certainly don't immerse yourselves in Britain's drug culture with remixes as your battering ram. Primal Scream wanted feeling from their recording time at Ardent and to a large degree that's precisely what they got.

Though a fine ten minute dance epic named after the album was put down, it was two ballads; the haunting 'Stone My Soul' and a cover of Beach Boy Dennis Wilson's 'Carry Me Home' that would be instrumental in moving them towards the next stage of their career. The songs poured with feeling, they were both broken and lusty and held a real sense of connection with the listener. The rich flavour of Big Star could be tasted thanks to their first class musicianship being emphasised wonderfully by the work of Weatherall and Nicholson. The songs were to be released on the back of the 'Movin' On Up' single under the moniker *Dixie Narco* EP.

Directed by Matthew Amos, a promotional video for 'Damaged' was filmed in a local tattoo parlour and captured Robert having a 'Heart And Soul' logo decorate his shoulder. Amos was also at the helm for another stylish performance clip that accompanied 'Movin' On Up' - the most commercially accessible track on the album. The production values of their videos were rising rapidly since their half-hearted attempt for 'Gentle Tuesday' and more recently the lazy, effects-drenched effort for 'Loaded'. Surprisingly, unlike so many artists who perceived themselves as serious musicians, it seemed as though Primal Scream now embraced the medium of music video, as in 'Movin' On Up' particularly, they threw themselves wholeheartedly into the intense physicality of a proper live show.

Back in the UK, a performance on the popular TV programme *The Word* was of great promotional value. It had emerged as a controversial magazine show, broadcast late on a Friday night, no doubt targeting an early twenties demograph; the same punters who read the music papers and wondered what on earth all the fuss was about. Distorted with amplification, Andrew's opening chords of 'Movin' On Up' had the smart young audience clapping in anticipation while Bobby, jumping and clapping with Jaggeresque élan, glowed in tight leather trousers and a wrinkled red shirt next to the ever-smiling Denise Johnson. Robert nodded approvingly behind his shaggy mane while enjoying his warped solo. The song was easily Primal Scream's most gleefully commercial and upbeat moment since the *Screamadelica* explosion and, packaged as the *Dixie Narco* EP, it duly received the biggest push from Creation hoping for its first top ten single. It failed by one place in January 1992.

A short tour around Europe exposed some cracks in the carnival, prompted by bad weather, confused audiences and frighteningly, some unwelcome attention from persons concerned not with the band's music but substances that had by now been glued to their reputation. Nevertheless the dates in Ireland revitalised the band in time for a four-week tour of America - it would be their first chance to perform there.

Ever aware of what was happening in America and clearly desperate to make an impact there, Bobby's thoughts on how his band would now be received by Americans could be assumed to be significant following the band's breakthrough domestically. Unfortunately though, the prospect of the land of opportunity failed to expose a kink in Gillespie's brash armour.

Prior to Sire releasing 'Loaded' he said: "I think our music will go down really well in America. You see, a lot of really bad British bands have kind of half made it in America and you just think, 'Well, what are they going to do when they hear us because we're so good.'" By February of '92 however, as he would later admit, things had changed. At the height of Grunge America was hardly ready for Britain's most fashionable dance rock pioneers, who themselves were very excited about performing in the country that gave birth to both rock 'n' roll and house music; the very genres that their current album had fused so successfully . Whatever the reaction, they were determined to have a good time.

While still traditional to the extent that everyone could understand at least part of the show, the handful of club dates largely failed to convince the commercial American market. Not that they were intended to do very much other than attract press attention of course and the shows were duly awarded some glowing, if often curious write-ups. Primal Scream did all that was asked of them and there were indeed some storming nights, not least in the more dance friendly arenas of New York and Chicago. Yet for America in the early 90s the band were, as they themselves have declared with a self-satisfied awareness, 'ahead of their time' and by at least five years at that.

Back home the ball was kept rolling with the release of *Screamadelica* the video compilation. It featured clips for nearly all the album's songs and behind-the-scenes footage of the previous year's UK tour. In addition they offered their own sightseer's guide to Memphis which, on further inspection, probably wasn't just a holiday souvenir but a parody of classic Elvis documentaries filmed in the same locations. It was plagiarism turned inside out as their groundbreaking sounds were juxtaposed by a great love of traditional American music light years from what was happening on Britain's dancefloors. Bobby Gillespie, it seemed, was determined to have it both ways.

While Robert and Andrew seemed content to remain in the background of photos, videos and only rarely gave interviews, it was left to the frontman to dominate the band's image. Six months since the album's release and with the advent of the successful and equally acclaimed *Dixie Narco* EP, Bobby kept his band's media profile impressively high. He was on magazine covers; sharing his opinions, reviewing music and was spotted hobnobbing with the likes of Kylie Minogue. Most importantly though, and now everyone seemed to agree, his band's music was helping the UK's independent music scene not only compete with that of the rest of the world but smash rivals into total indifference.

On the live trail, euphoric performances and all-night epics at the Brixton Academy and the Hammersmith Palais, clearly proved that for the country's sizeable population of students Primal Scream threw the finest concert money could buy. The date at the Palais, it was rumoured, was where Miss Minogue had first tried ecstasy. It was one of the year's few representatives in a 1996 feature in *Q* magazine entitled 'The One Hundred Best Gigs Ever'. Everyone was flying.

At Glastonbury they gave perhaps the finest performance in their entire history. Powerful and devastating, it was a truly great night as they were rewarded by an ocean of clapping hands stretching as far as they could see. Of all the artists playing the famous festival that year the reviewers were left with little doubt who was best, as Primal Scream delivered a set that was faithful to their album, yet intense, compact and highly aggressive. The performances throughout the whole tour had more or less been convincing and, quite rightly, it filled the band with pride when their *esprit de corps* came to the fore, as Andrew hinted to Kylie during a famous cover story for *Select*: "It happens once in a concert, when we all look round and catch each other's eyes and for us it's the greatest high - because there are eight of us."

On hearing the album, the listener could be forgiven for assuming that perhaps the sounds could not be recreated very well for the stage - having been born largely from studio technology, but thanks to some skilful improvising seeing the *Screamadelica* material performed live in '92 was every bit as authentic as the songs from *Primal Scream* had been three years previously.

The year ended well, as they had the honour of being awarded the much-hyped inaugural Mercury Music

Prize. Primal Scream beat off competition from the likes of Simply Red as a panel of respected judges decided that *Screamadelica* was the finest British long player of the preceding year. Bobby professed not to care about the ceremony, at London's swanky Savoy Hotel, where a spoof band representative known only as 'The Archbishop' collected the gong. There was still a party to celebrate though, one that was wild enough to see them somehow lose the prize money, as by morning the twenty thousand pound cheque was nowhere to be seen. Embarrassed, they appealed to Mercury to make them out a new one... The publicity surrounding the award quickly saw the album back on the chart more than a year after it was released.

In what would be their final concert in Britain for eighteen months, Primal Scream then performed a charity show at the Sheffield Arena. The mineworkers made redundant in the 1980s by the despised Tory Government were now the beneficiaries of a show that also included The Orb. A phenomenal twelve thousand fans turned out ensuring it was a huge success with bassist Peter Hook of New Order joining them for a stunning rendition of the Joy Division classic 'Atmosphere'. The concert raised nearly forty thousand pounds.

Following the weather, and in buoyant mood, there

was then a short tour in the baking summer heat of Australia and Japan that was cheerfully relaxed and not totally intent on promotion. It seems only appropriate that the end of this era was marked with the most original of hotel assassinations; one which involved a guitarist wearing only a cloud of fire extinguisher foam and nonchalant sunglasses. They covered the bill of course, Primal Scream always do, they're considerate people, while Alan McGee put his finger on why he knew he finally had the most chic band in Britain: "See, the thing about them is they're honest. Whatever they're feeling at the time is what they're going to do. We were all going to clubs around '88, '89 and that's why *Screamadelica* happened."

give out...

So where could Primal Scream go after the masses of acclaim that had followed the album, live performances and refreshingly honest attitude? Suddenly, for the first time in years, here were bands such as The Stone Roses and Primal Scream who spoke their minds and told it precisely like it was. Bobby was always protective against any criticisms though and, predictably, not everyone shared in the rejoicing of an attitude which had united so many, creating such a warm and welcome movement. Attacks on the band flooded the letters pages of the UK music press with the subject more often than their apparent endorsement of illegal drugs.

However it may seem, Primal Scream have never told anyone to try drugs. When asked about the use of substances, Bobby would answer any questions honestly and for a time seemed especially interested in discussing their influence. While never once ignoring the obvious risks involved, referring to past experiences he explained many times how the resulting feeling was something that a lot of stiff and short-sighted people should be aware of before telling others what they should or shouldn't do.

"When I first took acid it reinforced a lot of things that I already believed," he said in a typical statement, "I would definitely proselytise for drugs any time, because people who use drugs wrongly, that's their problem. If you've got a brain then you're okay with drugs. Give people the choice, that's what I say. Don't infringe on anybody's personal liberties."

Everyone had already heard many times about the appeal of getting high, so it wasn't as if exposure via a pop group who'd just recently sold their first couple of hundred thousand albums went a long way to spreading the word. Deep down the band blamed selected sections of the press for portraying them in a derogatory way and relationships with certain journalists became fragile.

Of course they used drugs, they never denied it and professionally they'd benefited hugely from the knock-on effects of their indulgences. Such was the success of their album, one that couldn't have been more obviously influenced by ecstasy if it was named after the drug (just notice the song titles) that unfortunately they soon gained a reputation for rather more than recreational hedonism. Even ten years after *Screamadelica*, when their public opinion of illegal drugs could be contradictory to say the least, in almost every article written about them there would appear some sly suggestion of them over doing it with anything from aspirin to nuclear poison. Time and time again they'd be written off, considered an inch away from death by needle, by writers who it seemed had forgotten that it's the music, and precious little else, that their opinions should be concerned with.

By '92 ecstasy was no longer the liberating force it had been, since the whole scene in the UK had been ruined by gangsters trying to create a more powerful version of the drug to make profits for organised crime. Primal Scream had tasted the highs and now it appeared that they were paying for their sins.

Years later, on hearing various band members discuss this period in possibly mischievous mood, it emerged that by then drugs may well have been needed to assist their work; cocaine was mentioned and so were harder drugs. While separating fact from fictional exaggerations always proves difficult with the band, Alan McGee has admitted that there were genuine problems.

By now Creation was financially secure and perhaps the most fashionable independent in the country. The success of Primal Scream saw them become the company's biggest band and accordingly this afforded Alan more than ever. He'd sold approximately half of the label to Sony Music, hoping that their next album would become a huge international seller with the power of the major assisting its promotion.

In finalising the deal, Alan has since admitted that much of his reasoning was that the success of *Screamadelica* ignited thoughts that they really could go on and become the biggest band in the world. Bobby Gillespie no doubt didn't care to be put under such pressure but, when announced, the connection with Sony was scorned by many with his band especially taking heat for reasons beyond their control.

Many claimed that as with 'Loaded' they'd betrayed their past, that going with Sony was yet more evidence of treachery, that Primal Scream had sold out on their way to an existence as yet another bloated rock band. Not that the prospect was without advantages, considering that Bobby had bitched back in 1990: "We used to get upset when people called us an indie band because all the other bands who were round at the same time as us always looked really dour and kind of ugly as well, and proud to be on an independent label. But if you look at any of our old interviews, we always said that we wanted to be a massive pop band."

So by late '92 he would have his wish, but Primal Scream would be playing a completely different ball game to the one they had enjoyed as reluctant leaders in the relatively unconstrained world of indie. Now, how they would exist as a small stubborn act in what was essentially a massive world of corporate back slapping would be interesting to say the least.

For a gang of fun-loving, working class friends who'd grown up and seen many lows together, the new income was, perhaps understandably, not used very responsibly. That winter they spent tens of thousands in the studio trying to record virtually a whole album of songs before they were fully written, and the lack of preparation resulted in a chronic waste of money as barely a song was completed. The new ideas sounded like the excellent work on The *Dixie Narco* EP and music similar to that on the second album, both a long way from their most recent long player. Notably, The Stone Roses, whose eponymously titled 1989 debut had been spoken of as a forerunner to *Screamadelica*, were themselves also struggling to record a follow up on a bigger label. Their blueprint could very likely be fully realised by the next, more powerful effort from Primal Scream, the equal jewel in a crown that had first shone because of William and Jim Reid.

Since the explosion of The Jesus And Mary Chain back in the mid 80s, through acts like The Smiths and New Order, the general perception of 'alternative' rock music among record-buying demographs had changed

Bobby Gillespie and Alan McGee were friends from their schooldays. As Alan formed Creation Records, Bobby dreamt of pop stardom with his newly formed band Primal Scream.

Yet it was Bobby who 'discovered' Jim and William Reid and the act that put Creation on the map - The Jesus And Mary Chain. Bobby made his public debut as both singer for Primal Scream and drummer for The Mary Chain at Glasgow's The Venue on 11 October 1984.

Gillespie's subsequent decision to quit the overwhelmingly successful JAMC for his own band would eventually serve him well.

Concurrently, Bobby and guitarist Jim Beattie were tentatively forming Primal Scream. Yet their emerging brand of sweet pop failed to inspire critics until a B-side, 'Velocity Girl', featured on the now infamous NME 'C-86' tape.

Douglas Hart, the Reid Brothers and Bobby prepare to terrorise the charts.

Bobby keeps time for the Reid Brothers

Alan and Bobby formed a close friendship that would eventually lead to a new era in British music.

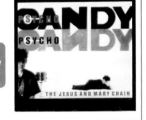

Primal Scream c.1986, with co-founder Jim Beattie bottom right.

Primal Scream's first offerings: All Fall Down & Crystal Crescent/ Velocity Girl.

Primal Scream's first two albums were met with critical disdain, yet they have since been credited as an inspiration for the subsequent explosion of British independent music.

1987's *Sonic Flower Groove* inspired a host of jangly imitators, and a track from their 1989 follow up, *Primal Scream*, was remixed with incredible consequences.

Bobby in leathers in 1989 and 1994 - his spell with long hair only broken by the Screamadelica period.

Primal Scream's first long players: Sonic Flower Groove & Primal Scream

Unknown DJ Andy Weatherall whose skills took Primal Scream to another level

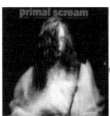

Loaded: the track that launched a thousand imitations

Bobby, in Sonic Flower Groove mode.

One of the finest albums ever made, 'Screamadelica' has been called the 'E-generation's Sergeant Pepper'

The recording of the 'Dixie Narco' EP took the band to Tennessee, the genesis of rock 'n'roll

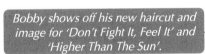

Bobby shows off his new haircut and image for 'Don't Fight It, Feel It' and 'Higher Than The Sun'.

The Scream team in their early 90s pomp - left to right: Martin Duffy, Robert Young, Andrew Innes and Bobby Gillespie.

The band's sojourn to Tennessee saw them record B sides for 'Movin' On Up' that would inspire them onto the next stage of their career.

The subsequent sessions for their next album, *Give Out But Don't Give Up* spiralled as the band sought the talents of producers George Clinton, Tom Dowd and a whole host of historic session players.

The resulting LP has since been criticised by its creators yet showed, via singles like 'Rocks' that the Scream could still produce good time tunes.

The extensive tour to support 'Give Out...' strained the band to its limits - here featuring Denise Johnson 1994.

Featured on the album were some of the greatest names in American music, not least 'Father of Funk' George Clinton

Ardent Studios drew the band to Memphis - the resu was 'Give Out...' an album criticisec for not being 'Screamadelica 2'

Bobby and Kylie enjoy a quiet lunch

Bobby on stage

Promoting *GOBDGU* was exhausting; taking in most continents, the band were touring constantly and the strain began to tell.

Bobby Gillespie's high profile image meanwhile catapulted him into the rarified atmosphere associated with a rock god, something to which he had always aspired.

Fame had reached a peak for Bobby and the band when this comic, featuring ex-Stone Roses bassist Gary Mountfield, appeared in Vox in September 1997

The band's fifth album 'Vanishing Point' brought critical acclaim. Sadly, the first tour to promote it proved a flop as the band discovered the studio based sound difficult to replicate live.

A new level of maturity marked the return of the band; their 3 year absence from the charts enabled them to sidestep the Britpop nonsense and return a sharper, more clued-up outfit. The subsequent tours in 1998 proved to be some of the most memorable of their career.

'Vanishing Point's inspiration was the 1971 film of the same name. Here, Bobby takes a car from the film - a Dodge Challenger - out for a spin.

Part-time genius Kevin Shields joined the band in 1999 following a critically acclaimed remix of 'If They Move, Kill 'Em'.

An album of remixes from 'Vanising Point', 'Echodek' was revolutionary, more proof that the band were willing to 'push the envelope'.

The new Primal Scream line-up, now with added 'Mani' 1997.

LONDON-12.8.01

DRESDEN
BOMB THE PENTAGON
SICK CITY
SHOOT SPEED
PILLS
BURNIN WHEEL
LONG LIFE
DOORS
BLOOD MONEY
ROCKS
KOWALSKI
ACCELERATOR
SWASTIKA EYES
KICKOUTTHEJAMS

Rocket Scientist Confidential   12/8/01   Page 1

n recent years Primal Scream have
ecome recognised as survivors.
'et age has not mellowed them,
heir most recent gigs providing
vidence of a new genre dubbed
disco punk', while their views on
ssues as diverse as world
errorism and drugs often leaves
oday's money-oriented groups in
ne shade.

hus as Primal Scream bask in their
orties, the punk ethic remains,
/hile their chameleon like
endencies to easily interchange
tyles continues to impress.

The band's last two albums have met with critical success.

The controversy surrounding this setlist and a new song entitled 'Bomb The Pentagon' only flared up once Al-Qaeda carried out the September 11th attacks. No one could suggest complicity on Primal Scream's part.

Critical acclaim has justified Bobby Gillespie's belief in himself. Some 19 years since he started making noise in a Glasgow bedroom, his band are perhaps the most respected of their generation.

00646

massively and for the better. Between '88 and '92, many of the teenagers who'd started bands after punk and had been further encouraged by The Mary Chain, acid house and a suddenly welcoming commercial radio, roared triumphantly in the press, on *Top Of The Pops* and finally populated the upper regions of the charts.

After years of lifeless synthesizers and equally emotionless stadium posers monopolising the mainstream, guitars were hip once more but with a dance edge. After Primal Scream, The Stone Roses and The Happy Mondays came the likes of EMF, The Inspiral Carpets, Jesus Jones, The Mock Turtles and Glasgow's The Soup Dragons. There was hardly a better time to be in a white guitar band as, post-Weatherall, every knob-twiddling DJ in town was aching to loosen up what four years before would have been considered impenetrable underground music.

But how, absolutely everyone was anxious to know, would this revolution of sorts develop? Primal Scream, while publicly expressing their approval of some of their contemporaries during this period, were never likely to get carried away with fads and set about pre-production on an album that, upon completion, they claimed was the one they'd always wanted to make. The guessing game continued as usual.

"What really makes us sick are the accusations of bandwagon jumping and the idea that many rock journalists have got into believing that Primal Scream are now basically a front for Andy Weatherall," ranted Bobby to *The Face* in '91. "I don't think Weatherall could have made records like 'Loaded' before he met us. It's like when people ask where we got the samples from for 'Come Together', we actually wrote those parts ourselves!"

While still basking in the glory of *Screamadelica*, Primal Scream's loose, experimental attitude that welcomed the contributions of the likes of Weatherall had become something of a double-edged sword, as their award winning album was often credited by the media to seemingly anyone but the band and, as Bobby explained, they were starting to find it hurtful. They were determined to do something about it.

They'd already decided to make the type of album that would be clearly all their own work because, as impressive as it was, *Screamadelica* was hardly a full band record in the traditional sense and definitely not a rock 'n' roll one. But after the exhaustion of the previous three years they couldn't seem to come up with anything new other than broken late night ballads and, while not being an especially serious problem, there can be little doubt that lethargy played a part in their lack of innovation.

"We were listening to a lot of Southern soul records," said Bobby of the period, "people like Otis Redding, James Carr, Percy Sledge. When we look at what music should be, we always go back to that stuff and to jazz: Ornette Coleman, John Coltrane..". And so, with a copy of *Screamadelica*, scruffy demos were speculatively sent to Tom Dowd, the sixty-six-year-old producer of soul legend Aretha Franklin and John Coltrane. Though he was somewhat confused by the album and having heard mere sketches of the band's ideas, Tom nevertheless jumped aboard without hesitation, something that flattered Primal Scream no end but still they needed more new material.

Bass player David Hood and drummer Roger Hawkins were hired with Tom's blessing; they were the legendary rhythm section from Alabama's famous Muscle Shoals studio and had played on classic songs by the likes of Willie Nelson and Wilson Pickett. The Memphis Horns duo of Andrew Love and Wayne Jackson would also play on the record as they had for the likes of BB King, Neil Diamond and Elvis Presley. These were historic musicians and despite being many years younger, Primal Scream truly believed that recording with them would take them one step closer to greatness. It was soon apparent that the whole thing was turning into a virtual who's who of Atlantic Soul, somewhat strange when one considers that Primal Scream hailed from urban Scotland but they could always feel the emotion of those records and that counted for a lot. With all these famed professionals willing to contribute to their album, the little band from Glasgow were nervous but very excited.

After a meeting in London, Ardent Studios was chosen as the location for recording, not only because of its traditions and the joyous experience they'd had there back in '91, but also the lack of temptation in surrounding Memphis. The place would restrict the possibilities of certain distractions for the self indulgent Primal Scream, who weren't exactly known for taking things easy. Still, in-between recording and overdue writing, there was the occasional mishap, the most serious of which threatened the very life of Martin Duffy.

During a break in recording, Robert and Martin visited New York to attend a music seminar and spent an evening getting inebriated at a forgotten watering hole. That night, possibly by falling on broken glass, Martin was stabbed by the kidney and some time passed before anyone noticed. Belated medical treatment revealed that the injury almost cost him his life but he fortunately made a full recovery which would have flawed the schedule, if not for Dowd. Flexing the muscles of his reputation, Tom acquired the talents of Jim Dickinson himself to fill in for a further take of a new song called 'Big Jet Plane'. Having the financial support to spend longer in the studio like this wasn't a problem per se, but it did allow irritating thoughts of even the slightest dissatisfaction to be tackled head on.

Although the task wasn't yet complete, the band clearly weren't going to get strained with the situation, and frequently rested until the right inspiration arrived. Near the end of their time in Memphis, some of the crew took time out and visited Los Angeles where they met George Drakoulias, the producer and bass player known for his work with The Black Crowes. George was impressed by Primal Scream's historical knowledge and Andrew in particular who had had a classic misadventure back in the South, at Graceland. Making some sort of pilgrimage to the home of the king would only be expected, but his gesture of vomiting on the grounds wasn't appreciated with any great affection...

"We realised that what we're good at is songwriting, playing, arranging but we aren't good at producing and mixing," said Bobby to David Cavanagh of *Select*. "We've always wanted to try and get good people to work with us but we never had the money and we used to get laughed at." Indeed, things weren't progressing as they would have liked with the mixing, and with deadlines looming - it was decided that now they had the money to take the difficult tracks elsewhere. It meant telling Dowd that they were moving on without him. Having been such an authority in the studio, Tom openly accepted their considering someone else to work on the post-production, while they insisted that as their main producer he'd done nothing but an excellent job.

Bringing the tapes back to the UK they found Andy Weatherall unable to mix the Bobby-less trio of 'Funky Jam', 'Give Out But Don't Give Up' and Denise Johnson's 'Free'. Instead it was arranged for the legendary George Clinton of Parliament / Funkadelic fame to take care of the troublesome tracks in Detroit where he even ended up singing on the former two. Although he never actually met the band, George clearly had an understanding of their music by the time he sent it back when Denise added further vocals to technically duet with him. 'Funky Jam' was then remixed by Paul Weller's producer Brendan Lynch into 'Struttin''.

By now though the project appeared in danger of becoming too elaborate and Alan was getting worried, but still that wasn't the end of it. The old desire for perfection had caused the schedule to slip which was the reason for Alan's concern, more especially considering that the profits made from what he'd put out since *Screamadelica* had only marginally recouped their overheads. With his most bankable act having lost focus somewhat via a stabbing, maybe a tad too much ambition, a heavy consciousness of their game plan and almost certainly one powder party too many, a pressure was building on what they came up with to, if not quite be a huge commercial success, then certainly recoup the mounting recording costs.

It was a conflicting issue that was hardly unusual between artists and their labels but Alan's faith in what they were doing, publicly at least, appeared to be total, with Bobby telling the press: "Like McGee says, you don't put any price on a great record. It's like, whatever it takes. I think we're giving him a great record and he's going to be proud to release it."

Always their most loyal supporter, Alan had seen his best friends grow up and become a truly meaningful UK act; well capable of delivering one of the most eagerly awaited albums of the year. Yet they were a business now and, inevitably, as often happens when money and egos grow prominent in rock 'n' roll, the old solidarity was weakening, with people on both sides later admitting that communication wasn't as clear as it should have been and that their lifestyles had grown radically different. Alan had a lot riding on the next Primal Scream LP and nearly twenty years of friendship was suddenly looking less significant when balanced against their increasingly polarised professions.

As he now had what was a conventional business to run, the fact that Alan was looking at production costs of several hundred thousand looked ominously unrecoverable from some of the mixes he'd heard. It's unlikely that anything was forced by his ultimate say so, but the band's decision to look elsewhere for enhancement of the single material was surely a relief, as Alan was only too aware of the limited attention span of those that really mattered: the record buying public. If profits were to be maximised, then it was deemed essential that Primal Scream were marketed as a hard hitting rock 'n' roll band, the type that could grab potential buyers as well as please their loyal followers. Tom Dowd's sugary mixes were unlikely to do both.

In an attempt to increase their commercial appeal and under the watchful eye of Andrew, George Drakoulias was hired to remix the three singles on the album; the strident 'Jailbird' and 'Rocks' and the gentle '(I'm Gonna) Cry Myself Blind'. They worked at the Oceanway Studios in Los Angeles, receiving a visit from the rest of the band to re-record 'Call On Me', a song they hadn't quite nailed in Memphis. Again they were very happy to involve their producer as much as they felt necessary. "We use producers as part of the band," said Bobby, "we couldn't produce ourselves. We need to work with other people, that's how it works for us."

Give Out But Don't Give Up was a real musicians' album. Since the joyous experience of the last tour Primal Scream, in their own words, 'got off on the energy of playing live' and subsequent jamming sessions resulted in the basis for the new album. The track listing was: 'Jailbird', 'Rocks', '(I'm Gonna) Cry Myself Blind', 'Funky Jam', 'Big Jet Plane', 'Free', 'Call On Me', 'Struttin'', 'Sad and Blue', 'Give Out But Don't Give Up', 'I'll Be There For You' and an untitled twelfth song soon dubbed 'Everybody Needs Somebody'. Everyone was anxious to know about the record as it had been more than two full years since their last new material.

The lead single 'Rocks' was an immense party track. The comeback song immediately earned comparisons with The Rolling Stones which, alongside Primal

Scream's reported lifestyle, seemed to confirm their apparent fixation with the band. Alan McGee: "People go on to me about 'Rocks' saying, 'it's just The Stones' but when did The Stones last sound as good as that? No one's saying it's not influenced by them but The Stones haven't made a record like that for fifteen years, so what's the problem?"

It was a song, it would seem, that couldn't be taken at anything other than face value. Strangely though, for some wildly mysterious reason, one or two assumed that 'Rocks' contained subversive social comment. With all the mentions of dealers, whores, teases and charlie etc, even Bobby himself was moved to comment that despite the coincidences, it was actually nothing more than a balls out party song and that people should only concern themselves with how it sounded. Technically, 'Rocks' sounded absolutely perfect, perhaps too much so but still, even from the first single the critics were sharpening their knives, ready to cut into an album that they hoped would prove that *Screamadelica* was nothing more than a fluke.

Matthew Amos directed a flashy performance video that featured the band in full concert mode; indeed they looked more like The Rolling Stones than Jagger and Richards had done for a long time. The throat grabbing appeal of 'Rocks' ensured a high chart position and it duly peaked at number seven; their first top ten hit. This despite both the influential television programme *The Chart Show* refusing to show the video because of the lyrical references to prostitution and over a hundred thousand sleeves having to be belatedly junked because of a printing error.

'Jailbird' was more of the same, a filthy strutting rocker. It began the album with a false start before re-introducing us to a confident Primal Scream circa 1989 - full of raucous rhythmic guitar, slamming drums and clichéd lyrics. It sounded fuller than anything they'd done before, as if they'd finally learned how to play their instruments melodically yet in a thoroughly crowd pleasing manner.

Beneath the fat mix was a highly attractive piece of music showing off both skill and self-assurance: 'Call On Me', coming midway through the record, is a knees-up singalong every bit as real as anything The Faces ever recorded.

Hipshakers aside, it was off round the sunny sprawl of Americana and Britain's famous R&B scene of the 60s, skilfully transported to modern dancefloors and the lonely bedsits of estranged lovers. '(I'm Gonna) Cry Myself Blind' was beautiful, as was the gorgeous country of 'Big Jet Plane'.

Consider what saved the second album from being a complete write-off wasn't just what Weatherall saw in 'I'm Losing More Than I'll Ever Have' but likewise the almost naked feeling of the haunting, hurt drenched sound of no fewer than four other numbers aside from the sub MC5s. Five years on their ability to write pure ballads was as strong as ever. On *Give Out...* they were hook-laden with piano and multi-layered guitars; meticulously arranged backing for Bobby's precise, wailing vocals. 'Sad and Blue' was self explanatory, and the closing two, 'I'll Be There For You' and 'Everybody Needs Somebody', were pure arm-around-the-shoulder soul.

The third element to this confident record was George Clinton encompassing the talents of Brendan Lynch and Denise Johnson. 'Funky Jam' was completely new ground for Primal Scream, a multi-layered, optimistic blast of American funk, it showed that they still had a desire to experiment and having Clinton at the reigns was a dream come true. He was the grand-master of this music and his voice, and that of Denise Johnson, added a certain authenticity to the song. In fact, the vastness of 'Funky Jam' was such that its sibling, Lynch's space jam of 'Struttin', was considered by many to be even better than the original. It spun around the speakers, holding and releasing tension with a stomping beat that ached for listeners to move in tandem. Then there was the title track: 'Give Out But Don't Give Up' was passionate, intense and like much of the album, far from what many bigots thought acceptable from a band with humble Scottish roots.

Undoubtedly, this ambitious set was the biggest record of their career. What counted in March 1994 was that critically, it premiered to reviews that understood the point of what they were trying to do. There can be no dressing up the bald fact that it failed.

Though *Screamadelica* had been hugely influential, Primal Scream wanted a record where they could attack their instruments in the traditional way, away from the remixes and samples that in the wake of their recent past had become a national cause célèbre. They had no interest in writing a direct sequel and it was fairly inevitable that anything other than such would be immediately dismissed, however musically accomplished. Listening back to the band down the years, both on vinyl and in interviews, it hardly comes as a surprise that they made an album as historically aware as *Give Out But Don't Give Up* but it was a notion that presently didn't sit well with Gillespie. He attempted to justify the perception saying: "People think 'Primal Scream, all they want to do is find some place in rock history and they'll be happy'. That isn't why we do music. I love being in the room and hearing Mr Innes and Mr Young playing their guitars, or Marty playing the keyboards. Sometimes they'll play really soulfully and it really moves me. Or, they can play rock 'n' roll, like 'Rocks', and it sounds like an aeroplane taking off. I live for that. That's why I'm in a group. That's why they're in a group." It cut no ice with the press.

'Dance Traitors' is what they were now called which, while partially true, is an accusation that sadly disguised much of the great work on the album which you could quite easily dance to regardless. One reviewer ironically wrote that they'd delivered the album of the year, just that the year in question was 1972. Painfully the *NME*, who were very grateful to have been granted a listen to 'Rocks' long before its release and then been overwhelmed by it, couldn't see its parent album worthy of anymore than a paltry five-out-of-ten. Its sister publication *Vox* was generous enough to award an equally indifferent seven.

Select however realised that the musicianship on the album and the undeniable fact that it sounded great was something to be applauded. Reviewer Adam Higginbotham awarded full marks, mentioning that: "While not quite as grittily authentic as Gillespie would hope, it's a superb, artful simulation of the past that's even better than the real thing: an animatronics version of everything you could want from the years 1970 to '72, in one conveniently accessible package." In *Q* Giles Smith wrote: "*Give Out...* is chiefly a collection of punchy and tidy rock 'n' roll songs and only two tracks come near to the slightly messier Primals of old. Plagiaristic obviously, but if you're going to plunder the past, you might as well do so with this kind of vim." He gave it a very respectable four out of a possible five stars.

From the band themselves, all the talk now was of how nobody could play anymore, that there was no feeling in contemporary music because it just wasn't 'real', as Andrew told an American magazine: "It should be about songs and when you look at all these modern rock bands they don't have any songs, and if they do, they just have one that they play over and over." Bobby then dryly nodded: "it's like the glorification of ineptitude."

Musically, *Give Out But Don't Give Up* was without question a superb album but it was so opposed to what people were expecting that nobody seemed to get it; it was Primal Scream paying their respects. It was an admirable display of bravery in many ways, them showing a complete disinterest in both other people's opinions and all current fashions. Yet the record displayed a maturity beyond their years, a maturity that impressed the likes of Tom Dowd and George Clinton and for all they knew it was going to sell millions of copies.

The sleeve prominently featured a twisted confederate flag, something that brought its own adverse publicity to the band who insisted that people had the wrong idea, again. The back cover featured a less than flattering shot of the late Eddie Hazel, the notoriously whacked out guitarist from Clinton's Funkadelic. 'Just who do these kids think they are?' was the question on everyone's lips; Primal Scream were British indie darlings and press favourites who, judging by their imagery and sound, were now attempting to break into America-friendly stadium rock. And at first, record buyers actually seemed to be swallowing it. First week sales were amongst the biggest of the year in Britain, charting the album at number two when equal figures would have easily been enough for a number one in less competitive weeks, but its performance soon slipped and a sense of anticlimax began to loom.

In an attempt to limit commercial damage to the record the band became media whores, forever using television and the entertainment press to maintain their profile, often going on the defensive after the frosty response to the album. They performed 'Funky Jam' for MTV in New York with George Clinton, Andrew referred to River Phoenix as 'lightweight' upon hearing that the young actor had died following a drug overdose, and then 'Jailbird' was allowed to be used in a widely shown television commercial for a famous denim company.

For a band who little more than two years previously rebelled against the music industry with their own style of tour and unusual release schedule, the game plan was swollen to say the least. They put their best foot forward but just weren't as successful as their egos suggested. Leather and fur clad, the long hair and sexually ambiguous posing was on display for the video to 'Jailbird'. The second single was only a moderate hit despite Amos twice cutting a semi-live performance clip that featured footage from early dates of the forthcoming tour.

A major international tour to promote *Give Out But Don't Give Up* was perhaps inevitable in the wake of the Sony deal but more importantly it was good for band morale. The appeal of Primal Scream as entertainers was now greater than ever, as the new album was, to quote Bobby, "a mixture of hipshakers and heartbreakers" and it was an absolute spectacle when brought to life in front of an audience. Though the much-loved *Screamadelica* material was by no means neglected, compared to the strutting glam stomp of the new numbers it seemed as though now it was music for the masses, as the experiments were pushed aside in favour of a traditional rock 'n' roll spectacular. Following some low key performances, the extensive UK leg was a total sell-out with drummer Steve Sidelnyk replacing Tomanov for the start of a haul that would see them perform around a hundred dates across the world stretching well into '95.

Seeing Primal Scream tour the UK and mainland Europe that spring brought to life the ghost of The Rolling Stones, in the early 70s, swaggering camp pomp. Despite the critics' judgements, this was certainly no bad thing as the carefully planned sets provided arguably the most complete concerts they would ever play. In Britain the venues had moved up from clubs to more conventional theatres where they would usually play up to a thorough fifteen songs a night. The stages, meanwhile, were decorated with streaming glitter that shone amongst the twin guitar attack and Bobby, now a visually striking frontman; his pale skin contrasting with his shoulder length hair looked as feminine as Patti Smith or Joan Jett.

As on the last tour he was a skipping fox of a singer

next to Denise Johnson, with whom he performed some superb harmonies and a well choreographed clap-skip-spin dance routine. Robert and Andrew were a blur of frizzy hair and shiny leather. With beefed up *Screamadelica* material that usually ended the show, their lead and rhythmic lines would mesh to distortion, powering the concerts into a high-kicking flurry of sexual energy.

Blustering on stage at Glasgow's Barrowlands on 2 April to a reception worthy of hometown heroes, Primal Scream performed what was arguably the finest date of the entire tour. A rousing 'Jailbird' was quickly followed by 'Rocks' and 'Movin' On Up' as the venue trembled from the attack of the band's water-tight glam rock theatrics as they whipped their audience into a frenzy of adoration. After the dance trance of 'Don't Fight It, Feel It', a perfect 'I'm Losing More Than I'll Ever Have' had the audience singing along to its every word. The evening ended with 'Higher Than The Sun' surging straight into 'Loaded', which by now featured vocals from Bobby eerily reminiscent of The Rolling Stones' 'Sympathy For The Devil'. The UK leg ended when they performed to almost fourteen thousand people over three nights at London's Brixton Academy, where they shared the stage with George Clinton and his twenty piece orchestra, the P Funk All Stars. Then, after a sprint round the clubs of Europe, it was time for the big push.

Throughout the 80s Depeche Mode were one of the few English bands who built up a huge following in America. By the start of the following decade they were one of alternative music's most popular groups and for almost three months in mid '94 were touring The States on the final leg of an excessively overblown and soul-destroying world tour. Primal Scream were allocated the opening band slot.

In hindsight, the decision to accept the offer was a mistake as Depeche Mode were calamitously falling apart and by then Primal Scream themselves were beginning to lose impetuous having performed the same songs over and over again. The chance to play in front of several thousand Americans was no doubt a convincing factor when agreeing to the tour, which pleased their US label and Depeche Mode's wiry singer Dave Gahan, who had somehow heard that they liked to groove. He told *Q*: "I like to party and they were fresh people to party with. We had fantastic times, sitting up till seven, eight, eleven in the morning, in my room..." Ironically, Depeche Mode's indulgencies were rumoured to have shocked Primal Scream, so much so that they began to hold back and resist some of the usual touring temptations. Gahan, it turned out, didn't hold back, as within a year of the tour his addiction left him literally within an inch of his life.

In many outdoor amphitheatres, and before capacities of up to twenty five thousand, Primal Scream played songs from *Give Out But Don't Give Up* with only the best intentions, as the album had all it took to be successful in the notoriously fickle American market. The big rock gestures were easily re-creatable while the sound was well suited to the venues, so there was no obvious reason why the band wouldn't take to audiences and vice versa. It was the commercialisation that rapidly ruined the atmosphere for Primal Scream, who were soon just going through the motions. For a band used to the intimacy of Britain's concert halls, the enforced aloofness of playing in the bubble that surrounds stadium groups prevented them from absorbing any intensity from audiences. As a support act playing second fiddle, they were only required to play for forty minutes and unfortunately were hardly appreciated by the thousands of teenage girls who wanted to see Gahan's tattooed torso that little bit quicker.

Behaviour of the irresponsible variety was quite inevitable but from Primal Scream on a long tour hardly surprising. Tales of illegal mass skinny dipping leaked, that were actually based on undeniable fact. On 31 May local police by the San Antonio river arrested a group of rowdy men in their underwear for creating a disturbance and damaging the police's patrol boat. A guitarist from Primal Scream was involved. As much of this chatter was reported in Britain, it was apparent that despite all the best pampering the band were definitely tiring. In an attempt to cure the boredom of the long hours travelling and waiting around, they took to playing table tennis and watching old films, apparently two classic rock star pastimes when things get bad.

At the Garden State Arts Centre in Holmdel, New Jersey, Andrew Innes had his amplifier decorated with a huge communist flag that he'd picked up in Prague earlier in the year. Under the stage lights, the flag was less than adored by those in the audience who'd actually managed to find their seats, and so for the remainder of their set Primal Scream were barely acknowledged, never mind appreciated.

During Depeche's set on the tour's last night in Indianapolis, certain band members took to letting off bottle rockets from the audience, causing great concern with the heavy-handed security and a riot almost ensued. It was just about the most exciting thing to happen during their association with The Mode. While everyone was agreed that their behaviour was good-natured, they also acknowledged that it had just been a mistake, a mismatch of headliners and openers. Primal Scream wanted to headline and they eventually got their opportunity.

In venues far smaller than those in which Depeche Mode had played, they stretched out and performed as before in front of their own followers. Sadly though, regardless of all the efforts of the band and their US label, commercial success was barely existent, as American sales of the record had only reached a fifth of those anticipated. Using the confederate flag and not displaying the track listing anywhere on the outer packaging was hardly a wise move for America, while their decision to tour there in such a way was one that they soon regretted: "I thought it was a worthless experience personally," conceded Bobby less than two weeks after it was over, "we toured with Depeche Mode, who are really good guys, but it was four separate dressing rooms, four separate limousines, four separate hotel suites. I couldn't do that. I don't think it did any good for us as a band."

Next stop was Japan; always one of their favourite places to perform. As proven on many occasions, far-eastern teenagers seem to adopt western culture with more vigour than those to whom it traditionally belongs. In a country where the perceived poisonous influence of rock 'n' roll was limited by early evening starts and strict behaviour regulations, Primal Scream's 'we're here to entertain' ethos landed like a bomb. As a result they were followed wherever they went, mostly by teenage girls, from restaurants to hotels, to the concert halls, amusement arcades and airports. Shopping trips, especially to the bohemian district of their beloved Shibuya, saw them besieged with gifts from fans, who, perhaps more than anywhere else on earth understood their affable human qualities.

It all proved too much for the private Andrew Innes, who ranted: "I hate Japan. I hate the food and the drink and the expense. In any other part of the world, all the hassle and problems bring us all closer together as a band. Japan just tears Primal Scream apart." Indeed, such was the level of attention, that Bobby was mystified by concern from fans who wanted more than the usual autographs he was always happy to sign. Apparently, rumours had breathlessly circulated Tokyo that the singer was suffering from a mysterious illness and some fans were genuinely worried about the state of his health. It transpires that in the build-up to their visit journalists from the Japanese rock press were under great pressure to deliver a story on the band, and if that meant a little exaggeration concerning their excessive lifestyle then so be it. They were tired but as healthy as ever.

Needless to say, the concerts were long sold out and though not being among the very best they would ever play, they still did enough to prove that in a very Primal Scream kind of way, such 'looseness' remained brilliantly entertaining. The Stooges' 'No Fun' was added to the set but that was by no means the only cover they played: Sly And The Family Stone's 'Don't Call Me Nigger, Whitey' and John Coltrane's 'A Love Supreme' often appeared in the encore, as did The Clash's 'Jail Guitar Doors'. Routinely promoting the album was getting tedious and it seemed that they were forever coming up with different ways to keep themselves amused, and just as well, as there was little good news on the horizon, only more travelling and more dates, meaning yet more time in the company of the same crew who'd been together virtually non-stop for four years. Perhaps their decision to make future tours short and sharp had already taken shape but they soldiered on, professionals to the very end.

Back in Britain they geared up for an appearance headlining the prestigious Saturday night at the Reading Festival. Joined by former Clash guitarist Mick Jones and, during 'Loaded', Dave Gahan on shocking harmonica, a sluggish set was delivered, far up in the cold, well away from the passion of the audience to whom the below par performance didn't seem to matter a whit. On stage Bobby's shiny rockgod hair looked like it had been hacked at with a pair of sheers, while the recently-married Robert Young pouted along as usual, unable to hide his blushes as a sloppiness saw them unconvincingly stumble along. Not surprisingly, the reviews were uncaring, with little mercy shown to Bobby's slurred and tardy vocals.

Away from the band, the entourage often graced the tiny Heavenly Sunday Social nightclub in London, where The Dust Brothers, Ed Simons and Tom Rowlands, had been causing a sensation as the resident DJs. The club was the brainchild of Creation publicist Jeff Barrett who was astute enough to pick up on the talented duo long before word nationally spread. Primal Scream commissioning them to rework 'Jailbird' had been a masterstroke. It was another step for Ed and Tom who'd first signed to Andy Weatherall's label nearly two years before. The Brothers soon found themselves the desire of every desperate guitar band akin to Primal Scream having Weatherall remix them half a decade earlier and, with their crunching rock sound splashed in standard DJ dance, the press had coined the phrase 'big beat' that almost guaranteed them a welcome from waiting

Scream crowds up and down the land. In October, after one heavenly night at the Heavenly Social, an unsavoury incident served as a reminder of the problems living in Britain in 1994.

It was the day of a major Criminal Justice Bill march when Bobby and some friends wound up back at Alex Nightingale's house and were allegedly loud enough for police to have received complaints. After protesting their innocence by demonstrating the volume to the plain clothes officers, Bobby and his manager were said to have been physically assaulted but thankfully there seemed to be no serious implications. Primal Scream then promptly continued onto yet another leg of the tour.

Having given up all efforts to maintain their aloof image to vainly promote the album, it appeared that on these outings Primal Scream were again playing for the sheer fun of it. Never was this more evident than when they were joined on stage by Paul Weller at London's Shepherd's Bush Empire for a poignant version of The Who's 'So Sad About Us', a song that had occasionally appeared in the set since their earliest days.

'(I'm Gonna) Cry Myself Blind' had been played throughout the year and to coincide with its release as a single, a video was shot that featured them passionately miming in an empty theatre. Perhaps because the clip was rarely shown, or just because the whole euphoria had died down, they found the single no higher than number fifty-one in the charts; a placing that called for appropriate action. *Top Of The Pops* producer Ric Blaxill offered them a slot on the show, which Creation were so keen for them to accept, that they spent ten thousand pounds on a chartered flight to ferry them from Dublin to London for the taping and then back to Cork for their next show the same night. Primal Scream though, the difficult boys that they were, just didn't quite see it like that.

Having played a sensational concert in Dublin the night before, a nasty hangover was particularly evident and a phone call at the last minute revealed there was 'a problem'. The band's cocksure excuse for non co-operation was because they considered themselves 'far too rock 'n' roll for Luton Airport', a necessary pitstop for the operation to run as planned. "We didn't show because we got so wrecked in Dublin the night before," said Bobby, "then we got phone calls saying 'you'll never work in this industry again you bunch of junkies...'"

When cheekily quizzed by the *NME* a spokesperson for the Airport soberly declared: "Luton is a modern airport with all the facilities you would expect....Primal

who? I'm surprised someone would be as sad as this."
On behalf of *TOTP* Blaxill stated that he too was "disappointed by their attitude" and while there were no
set rules on banning artists from the show, after the
incident people could "draw their own conclusions."
The band's TV plugger was so furious that he
promptly resigned.

The long and exhausting tour ended in Australia and
the Far East. The performances at Australia's revolving
'Big Day Out' festival were disappointing and in their
reports for the British press journalists didn't pretend
that they were exposed to anything other than a tired
and disinterested band. When it was all finally over
Primal Scream were barely heard of for two years, an
absence which gave breath to rumours that, in the
wake of Britain's next press-hyped fad, they were
finished.

Just before Christmas, The Stone Roses had finally
released their second album, some five years after their
sparkling debut had bedazzled a generation. Bobby
famously announced in the *NME* that the preceding
single to their *Second Coming* album, titled 'Love
Spreads', was the greatest comeback song of all time. In
a strange act of fate, when recalling many of the
reviews of *Give Out...* that called the record some sort

of homage to The Rolling Stones, the new Roses album would suffer a similar critical doom. Accusations of Led Zeppelin imitation plagued *Second Coming*, suggesting perhaps that the cocky zest of both The Roses and Primal Scream had started some sort of trend, that at the very least could open a niche for some young students of rock mythology to march in and clean up. In retrospect, the writing was clearly on the wall.

More than a year previously, Alan spotted a band from Manchester called Oasis performing in Glasgow and liked what he saw. On the spot he offered them a multi-album deal and saw their debut LP *Definitely Maybe* launch them to national stardom. Within two years Oasis were multi-million selling and genuinely one of the biggest bands in the world. For better and worse, things at Creation would never be the same again.

vanishing point

The trend of indie guitar bands making dance records lasted about as long as the drugs were pure; most found themselves too stoned for the all-important follow up. Predictably, by the mid 90s, the charts were ruled by boy bands: their flashy dance moves and hidden producers polishing them for the gullible teen masses. When the next cluster of 'saviours' suddenly started selling, many of them had actually been around the circuit since the turn of the decade, but rather than emerge with talk of inspirational drugs or punk rock stars, the names getting dropped were the likes of The Beatles, The Small Faces, The Who and The Kinks, rather than 80s smoothies like say Dire Straits or Genesis.

After acclaimed albums by newcomers Suede and Elastica, major labels could no longer ignore the commercial potential of this retro rock, and just as *Sonic Flower Groove* had arrived a year too early for a perfect Madchester fitting, it turned out that *Give Out But Don't Give Up* came out just before this similar imitative music was being plugged by everyone from the majors to campaigning politicians; it generated

Britain's most celebrated and patriotic music scene since punk some twenty years before.

'Britpop' was huge. Because of that term, masses of guitar bands suddenly benefited from what was actually an age-old fad. In Primal Scream's absence many acts, including the distinctly British Pulp, Blur and Oasis all became platinum sellers propelled by the stirring, super-enthusiastic and highly influential music papers.

Select magazine, launched at the height of Madchester had, despite a novel and highly literate style, not quite reached its potential as that era's bands had all but ground to a halt while faceless dance music was unexpectedly holding the public's attention. Carrying the torch for the likes of Primal Scream during its first couple of years, when the wind of change finally blew it was perfectly placed to become a thriving, envelope pushing bible of happening guitar acts in the same way that the *NME* had attempted with its C back in '86. For all involved it had taken a decade of hard work, talent and incredible luck for that seed to spawn Britpop's self-righteous monster.

Everywhere you looked there seemed to be gangs of scruffy, mop-topped poseurs, desperately hoping to be part of this so-called movement. Summer festivals, for so long bohemian hippy hangouts, were suddenly the shows to not only play at but equally be seen loitering around backstage. Noticeably, the word 'indie' was now being used to describe a band's image rather than the independence of their label. It had become almost as major as everything it would have been independent of during the previous two decades.

One overnight success, the near satire act Menswear, had fluked a fledgling career and the accompanying press hype with the sort of luck that a court jester would be hard pushed to muster. Their fortune saw them able to release a rather unremarkable song called 'Stardust' that was hardly a tribute to David Bowie. The character identified in the lyrics is called 'Bobby', who's 'such a superstar', 'full of bravado', 'wears leather trousers' and has 'sold his soul for his rock 'n' roll and fame'. Correct guesses as to the song's inspiration will win no prizes.

And it wasn't just the upstarts benefiting from all the flag waving either as in, it has to be said rather embarrassing circumstances, even The Sex Pistols had suddenly decided to dust off their ill-fitting leather jackets and rusty safety pins and regroup for a world tour. All their live-fast, die-young bravado of twenty years earlier was suddenly forgotten at best and contradicted at worst; the appeal was apparently not the filthy lucre but because it was fun and they could do as they pleased. In all cases being a British musician of any standing in the mid 90s was a licence to walk taller and party harder.

An act unquestionably a cut above the rest were The Charlatans, who had first emerged as the 90s began with dance friendly rhythms similar to those connected with The Stone Roses and Primal Scream of the same period. To perhaps an even greater extent than Primal Scream, they too had so far persevered through a decade of professional and personal turbulence that was already praiseworthy, but when their keyboard player was tragically killed in a car accident, their slate was indefinitely wiped clean. Martin Duffy was drafted in as a studio and brief live replacement; a collaboration that, as you might expect, fed rumours that he'd soon make the move permanent. Rumours that turned out to be untrue.

Give Out But Don't Give Up almost sold a million. The help of Sony Music was no doubt a contributory factor to the extra sales as, until the lauded *Screamadelica*, their albums had barely registered on any chart. Although *Give Out...* was a conventional success; recouping its recording and promotional expenses that were estimated to be up to a million pounds combined - the album was considered a failure not only by much of the press but eventually even its own creators.

"*Give Out...*was quite disgraceful really," Bobby told *Raygun* three years after it came out, "I think we had a good idea, but I just don't think we nailed it properly. We were kind of off-focus, kind of displaced. It was a real downer record, real dark and ragged - there were only two songs that captured any kind of feeling." The feeling was certainly there; their reaction to the whole *Screamadelica* euphoria was one of collapse, tiredness and ragged emotion.

It was the classic criteria for a late night album but that very concept was thought over too long and too hard. While by no means a failure as a piece of music, when the dust had settled, it was hardly a worthy follow up to the genre-busting classic that had kicked down doors and united music lovers from opposite ends of the spectrum. By cynical comparison, *Give Out...*was simply an over-produced homage to records that Primal Scream loved.

Sony were disappointed. Though a successful album for Primal Scream, *Give Out But Don't Give Up* didn't prove to be quite the smash their new parent company had expected. If there was a glimmer of hope amongst the sense of failure though, it had to be that the real media interest in the band had only seriously begun five years previously and since then they'd proved that they would take their music anywhere people might want to hear it. Following a well-deserved period of recuperation, there was every reason to expect that from Primal Scream, who were still young enough, there would be further attempts to gain more substantial international success. Meanwhile Oasis were going a long way to covering Creation's debt with some monstrously successful singles on the back of the label's first-ever number one album. If they still existed then, for the time being at least, Primal Scream and every other act on Creation were forgotten as the five-piece from Manchester ruled supreme.

For Primal Scream there were departures from the camp. Touring bassist Henry Olsen left before any further daylight, as did drummer Steve Sidelnyk. Denise Johnson returned to Manchester and soon commenced working on solo material and collaborated with Michael Hutchence and Electronic. Of Primal Scream she said: "I'm not doing any work with them. I'm too busy myself. A lot of people have said I'll be sadly missed but that's how it goes. Even though I've got my solo career going, I'm still going to work with people that I think are credible and have something to offer the music world." Her own songs, the acclaimed 'I Believe' and 'Inner Peace' would briefly be released before bad experiences with record labels saw her promising career unintentionally stall. Denise's talents wouldn't be required further by Primal Scream but any suspicion of the parting being acrimonious should be quashed, as she would often be anonymously in the audience whenever they played Manchester in future.

Looking back on the *Give Out...* era, it's easy to see that Primal Scream had become a bloated version of their former selves and to Bobby, always the most vocal about his love of the band, this must have been a trifle embarrassing. The extra income afforded by the success of the album clearly meant little as he made no effort for attention for nigh on two years. He was the last of the brotherhood to move up to London, deep down considering if his group could ever again be a great as they had once been, and if they couldn't, then he just didn't see any point in continuing.

"I was feeling kind of worthless for quite a long time, because I wasn't actually able to do anything in my life that I was proud of and it seemed pretty endless," he later said of his missing years. But a desire to get back to work, and maybe even repeat the whole thing again, eventually proved too alluring to someone who had known nothing but making music his entire adult life.

As he explained in 2000: "We did a twenty-two week tour. It was debilitating and too one-dimensional.

I remember thinking: 'I don't want to do this any more. We have to change or die.' Basically, we took a year and a half off, deconstructed Primal Scream and started again."

Primal Scream are consciously very lucky people. All they have to do to earn a comfortable living is write, record and promote songs. By any definition it's not especially difficult. In the past, hardly any of the expense of this had come directly out of their pockets and they'd taken full advantage of the prestigious position they were in. Having come from ordinary backgrounds, they knew full well they were living a life of which their peers could only dream. They'd kept going through years of struggle for an absolute pittance but it didn't matter to them because they were doing something they absolutely adored. Playing everywhere from underground clubs to American sports arenas had been a spectacular journey and on it they'd lived up to their fortunes by often behaving in a way the world had come to expect of its trendy musicians. They'd extroverted themselves to an extent that it almost killed them, but by the time their mid-thirties came around all that was left to do was make more challenging music. It was all that mattered, well above the fluff that had recently threatened to suffocate them for good.

Primal Scream first met writer Irvine Welsh on tour, when he interviewed them for a magazine. Welsh was about to become the voice of a generation as his cult novel *Trainspotting* was being made into a film that would go on to become a phenomenal success; an accurate portrayal of the hedonism of mid 90s Britain. The writer approached the band to contribute to the soundtrack of the film, for which they duly composed a scenic instrumental that became the title track.

Bobby: "It gave me a lot of faith - it made us all feel proud. When you suddenly end up creating some music that's exciting and new and quite experimental, you start feeling a sense of self worth again."

Mixed by Andy Weatherall, the eponymous 'Trainspotting' was perhaps underplayed in the movie, while other, brasher numbers by the likes of Iggy Pop and Underworld accompanied scenes that some suggested glamourised theft and drug abuse. Inevitably, the film was heavily criticised, and closer to home the dangers of drugs were more obvious than ever, as Alan had suffered himself. During his enforced lay-off, thanks to Oasis, Creation had become the highest-profile record label in the country. But this was of little interest to Primal Scream as they were slowly getting back into gear.

Welsh took over lead vocals for Primal Scream's only original material released in 1996, a single jokingly designed to spur on the Scottish football team during the European Championships. Imaginatively titled 'The Big Man And The Scream Team Meet the Barmy Army Uptown', it wasn't the most sensible release of the summer, albeit a limited edition one. Welsh's foulmouthed lyrics over artificial terrace chanting and a hip-hop drum beat ensured that the amusing number was quickly dismissed by the press, who again rubbished the band for irresponsible laziness.

Humorously one hopes, the song was offered to the Scottish Football Association and they could hardly have been surprised when it was rejected. Instead the SFA opted for a number by that other football-mad Scotsman Rod Stewart, who would have been aware of Primal Scream by this point, as the year previously they had quietly contributed 'Understanding' to a Small Faces tribute album. Bobby Gillespie was noticeably absent from both 'The Big Man...' and 'Understanding', with vocals on the latter performed by modish 60s songstress PP Arnold. Still, he was happy enough to pose for a *Melody Maker* cover to publicise the football single; it was one of his few press appearances of the year.

Mr Welsh was by now a bona fide boozing buddy of

Primal Scream and their relationship developed further still when they were asked for a song for another movie adaptation of his writings called *The Acid House*. Though nothing was cast in stone, it appeared that every piece of new music they could muster was dark and paranoid. 'Insect Royalty', which they donated to the project, was a sleaze funk epitome of just where they stood. Without the prestige of *Trainspotting*, *The Acid House* would still stand above the slew of Britflicks that quickly sprang up, one of which, *Boston Kickout*, came with a hip soundtrack featuring Joy Division, Oasis, and their very own 'Loaded'.

Along with the trauma that comes with losing founder members, The Stone Roses were getting slammed by critics who somewhat harshly claimed that they were old hat in this hip climate. Those who remained from the quartet that was largely responsible for beginning the Britpop movement that was currently crushing them: singer Ian Brown and his loyal bassist Mani claimed all the adversity would be proven wrong by their appearance at the Reading Festival. It wasn't to be and with an air of inevitability The Stone Roses ended soon afterwards.

It had been a morale-draining five years since their

breakthrough album and, when they returned with a follow up, one of their following live dates was in Primal Scream's then home base of Brighton. Not surprisingly, the Scream contingent attended the show and were impressed. Mani meanwhile was privately disgruntled with what had become of his band and looking ahead enquired about the availability of the four-string post in Primal Scream; where there had been no full-time bassist since Robert back in '88. The response he received was affirmative. Mani was thirty-three and given a golden second chance.

Bobby: "I've known Mani since about 1989, up in Manchester, got on pretty well with him and I used to go and see The Stone Roses play and I really loved their band. On their last tour he kidnapped me in Brighton and took me to Newport. On that journey we had a really good talk, we had such a lot in common, politically, musically, attitudes, just everything."

Mani also concedes an affinity: "Glasgow and Manchester are twin towns and it turns out that Bobby was at the same gigs in Glasgow as I was in Manchester, so we kind of shared a similar musical heritage anyway."

'Mani' was born Gary Mounfield in Manchester, the city where he befriended Ian Brown in the early 80s and joined him in The Stone Roses on bass by late '87. Having met Bobby a short time later, he'd kept a close eye on Primal Scream, being most impressed by their renowned passion for music and living life to the full. If the solid bassist from The Stone Roses couldn't have continued as he wished, then joining Primal Scream was the very next best thing, as the parallels between the two had at times been uncanny.

Though easy to say in retrospect, *Sonic Flower Groove* sounded remarkably similar to *The Stone Roses* LP that was released not two years later and, consciously or not, both bands discussed comparable issues during interviews and had come to prominence with the rise of ecstasy used for recreation. Despite their status as underachievers, The Roses are thought of with great affection by Britain's indie kids, particularly those who lived through their late 80s heyday. Subsequently, the scattering members carried a considerably legacy into their future careers and, at times, the baggage got too heavy. Primal Scream, it seemed, were not remotely threatened by Mani's down-to-earth celebrity and welcomed his enthusiasm with open arms. Mani is an intelligent, highly approachable character and in addition to his musical usefulness it appeared that he didn't mind talking to the press. When news of his recruitment was made public it assured fans that

Primal Scream would be returning after a lengthy absence.

Bobby, Robert, Andrew and Martin had demoed new ideas in the dance music Mecca of Ibiza. After the misunderstanding caused by the last album, music closer to the style of *Screamadelica* was intended, which had started to come to life in their recently purchased studio in London's Primrose Hill with producer Brendan Lynch. Sex Pistol Glen Matlock was temporarily recruited to help with bass recording, while new drummer Paul Mulreany came aboard full time. Though not as extensive this time around, outside contributions to the recording also came in from Jamaican dub legend Augustus Pablo on melodica, while The Memphis Horns made a welcome return, as did once permanent guitarist Paul Harte, this time on harmonica and droog synthesizer.

The sessions were nowhere near as exhaustive as those for *Give Out But Don't Give Up*, with the band making tidy progress well into the autumn. Having tired of their traditional instruments, the musicians relished the opportunity to switch over in an attempt to keep the process of writing and recording from being the labour it had been last time; Robert experimented on keyboards and sitar, Andrew dabbled on bass while Martin also found himself on the melodica. It was a tactic that had benefited many bands in the past and Primal Scream found it equally therapeutic to experiment in a similar way to the sessions for *Screamadelica* five years earlier.

Since overseeing Weatherall's work on 'Loaded' those years before, Andrew Innes had by now come into his own in the studio. He would be the first to take the initiative; plan arrangements and supervise mixes. His work ethic soon infected everyone, as his vision of how the album would turn out came together solidly, without any input of powder, pill or puff.

If *Screamadelica* captured them on a drug-fuelled high, then the comedown, so to speak, had proved their downfall for the follow-up. Now, three years on, a fifth album was being made by an older band who were primarily focused on music. While Bobby's lyrics would attempt to shed light on the troubles of recent times this was, by and large, the start of a whole new era. News on the progress of the record was scarce to say the least as, following the announcement that Mani would latterly be joining, nothing further was heard until the spring. The new bassist recalls: "I never even heard anything until the day I turned up at the studio, they go, 'right, we've got this track called 'Kowalski', we're rolling the tapes, make something up'."

Vanishing Point **was one of the** first American movies made cheaply in the wake of the success enjoyed by *Easy Rider*. Directed by Richard Sarafian and released in 1971, it followed the story of Kowalski, a former racing driver, who takes up the challenge of driving from Denver to San Francisco in a Dodge Challenger, to meet a seemingly impossible deadline. Racing across the desert having consumed a mountain of amphetamines, Kowalski is encouraged by a pirate radio DJ to the annoyance of the pursuing police. As an avid lover of cult cinema, Bobby said *Vanishing Point* was highly appealing to the band but they thought that the music could have been better. So, perhaps in an attempt to re-write the soundtrack for a little-known American road movie that was more than twenty-five years old, Primal Scream had created album number five.

"The first time I saw it was about three years ago, the bloke in the film is driving a car at a certain speed and the tour bus we were driving was going at a speed, so it was like double speed, double motion all the way," Martin told a cover story for *Select*, while Bobby explained: "That's why we wrote 'Kowalski', because the soundtrack, we felt, didn't suit the feel of the movie. We thought we'd try and make the right music. That was the challenge, something that captures the feel, the paranoia, the amphetamine, the claustrophobia."

Named after the film, *Vanishing Point* the album would feature eleven tacks; 'Burning Wheel', 'Get Duffy', 'Kowalski', 'Star', 'If They Move, Kill 'Em', 'Out Of The Void', 'Stuka', 'Medication', 'Motorhead', 'Trainspotting', and 'Long Life'.

The publicity to promote the album saw the band cleaned up and revitalised. Mani couldn't stay quiet in interviews; right away he introduced himself as someone who had trouble keeping his opinions to himself. From the very start of his Primal Scream career he was their mouthpiece to the press, often announcing that he was now in the best band in the world and how grateful he was to his new colleagues for presenting him with a second lease of life.

Bobby on the other hand appeared much quieter, no longer aching to let off steam about many of the things that had concerned him beforehand, including drugs. Having reverted back to his '91 style fringe, he moodily avoided giving on-camera interviewers an easy time, often just passively nodding behind his wraparound shades, but he did manage to tell *Melody Maker*: "We really enjoyed making *Vanishing Point*. We went to the studio every day and just experimented with sounds and ideas. There's such a joy there, that's

why it sounds so alive. There's intensity of focus too -
musically, lyrically, attitude-wise, everything. The
clarity of thought is incredible on this album..."
Andrew, meanwhile, had retired from publicity
completely and on mandatory television appearances
would disguise his newly shorn head by wearing a
fighter pilot's helmet. It was a gimmick first seen in the
stunning promotional video for 'Kowalski'.

Directed by Steven Hanft and written by Irvine
Welsh, the clip featured supermodels Kate Moss and
Devon stealing a Dodge Challenger, attacking various
domino-playing band members and leaving them to
evaporate into thin air. A cross between the TV show
The Sweeney and the movie *Faster, Pussycat! Kill! Kill!*
was the apparent brief. If not quite pantomime, as a
promotional tool it was a great success, presenting a
light-hearted view of the band that hadn't quite been
seen before.

The song's feeling of movement wasn't lost on Bobby
who, although not actually able to drive himself,
apparently loves being in the passenger seat when a
car is moving at speed. Mani was given a credit for
co-writing, as the song heavily featured his machine
gun bass along with distorted space noises, samples
from the film's DJ character Super Soul played by
Cleavon Little and Bobby's cool whispered vocals.

Reviewers likened it to being in the cockpit of a plane speeding up a runway, while members of the band declared it the sound of 'a junkyard having a nervous breakdown'. The hype surrounding 'Kowalski', their first proper single in years, saw it become their biggest-ever hit when it charted at number three.

'Burning Wheel', the opening number, was a psychedelic tour of the inner thoughts of one of Bobby's most distraught characters yet. He sang of diseased eyes and being a thief; it was always going to be a highlight - a blissful combination of fat beats and echoing guitars. It contained all the best elements of the drug-sounding era of Primal Scream, wrapped in a Pink Floyd-esque trip round a disturbing world of cinematic paranoia. For establishing a late 90s mark of the band, it was a remarkably modern sounding song, and a fine call to arms to the rest of the album. On numerous occasions Bobby called 'Burning Wheel' easily the best thing they'd ever done and if he wasn't deadly accurate with his declaration, then he was pretty close.

The 'chemically imbalanced' individual he sang of during 'Out Of The Void' appeared to represent diametrically opposite feelings to those generated by 'Higher Than The Sun'; it was a disturbing and, as Bobby readily admitted, revealing portrait of the pain felt from recent wounds. Quickly followed by the dub inspired madness of 'Stuka', it was clear that while much of *Vanishing Point* was thematically an obvious relation to *Screamadelica*, its message was concealed within a far less celebratory tone. It was a focused, dark and difficult listen; a poisoned retreat from their early 90s rapture. It was also an unpredictable record and quite possibly their most surprising release yet. Unconventional percussion sounds and random instrument stabs flew around the speakers, piercing a swirl of burning basslines, synth breaks, guitar attacks and deep, multiplying vocal noises. The luxury of their own studio had been optimised fully during the recording and mixing, a novelty that presented them with an opportunity to display a sense of humour more directly than ever before.

'Motorhead' was a wild digital sprint across Lemmy Kilmister's band's namesake while 'Medication' saw them return to their Stones-esque best; a hangover from the last album maybe but still a swaggering slice of classic glam regardless. Again, Bobby explicitly barked the type of lyrics that left few gaps for the listener to fill. 'If They Move, Kill 'Em', named after a line of dialogue from Sam Peckinpah's film *The Wild Bunch*, was a jazz funk explosion that made excellent use of horns. Its thumping bass, it was felt, needn't be tarnished by vocals so it remained an instrumental, likewise 'Get Duffy'; a tinkering cocktail of pure sunshine relaxation. The sweet singalong of 'Star' featured Bobby's most obviously political lyric to date, and 'Long Life' was a beautifully drifting outro. *Vanishing Point* was a fascinating listen, and one that nobody was prepared to let pass unnoticed.

During a press visit to America a video for 'Star' was shot in South Central LA starring Mani who, being vulnerable to the odd initiation ritual, was apparently ordered to act out a hilarious chase sequence. The success of the song was also helped by live performances on TV shows such as *Later With Jools Holland* and *Top Of The Pops*, bosses at the latter having obviously forgiven the frustrating day of wasted negotiations back in '94.

That summer also saw the release of the book *Primal Scream Higher Than The Sun* by Grant Fleming. Fleming was the band's T-shirt seller and in-house photographer between 1990 and 1995. The book was an often hilarious collection of memoirs of all the on-the-road partying, aptly illustrated by his holiday snaps and frantic writing style. Though the overall tone of the book is delightfully comedic, Grant occasionally hints at some discontent within the camp, which said much about the actual seriousness with which they take their profession. It was a fascinating look at a less than glamorous part of their lives and, for a fan, as a behind the scenes document of the band in the heady first half of the 90s it was a fitting memento.

Though some way behind first week sales of The Prodigy's *The Fat Of The Land*, *Vanishing Point* entered the charts impressively at number two upon its release that July. Also, and not surprisingly, the *Vanishing Point* movie was re-released onto the home video market, newly packaged with the inevitable sticker explaining that the containing feature had inspired one of the most eagerly awaited records of the year.

Expectations for Primal Scream's first live performances in more than two years were huge. The reviews of the album had been very favourable, as everyone seemed to agree that after the relative letdown of the last album, they'd put to rest fascinations with their influences and concentrated on what they were so good at.

Several reviewers claimed that in places *Vanishing Point* hit the heights of *Screamadelica*, while others rated it their best effort yet. *Select*: "With *Screamadelica*, Primal Scream were a band with only one place left to go - too far. Now it seems they've got there. Five-out-of-five." *Q*: "Put simply, they still have great record collections and an uncanny talent for bottling the essence of whatever genre they decide to dabble in. Four-out-of-five." None of the chiefly impressed writers were brave enough however to speculate on just how this transfixing record would be performed live. It was a question that couldn't be fully answered for some time.

They'd provided teasers of their new set by performing on a boat sailing down the Thames in front of a select few and even did a low-profile set in the dance tent at Glastonbury. However the real thing got under way in Europe and things didn't start well at all. Firstly, two members of the band's entourage were arrested in possession of illegal substances, drummer Paul Mulreany inexplicably left and then all dates on the short UK tour were postponed with no satisfactory explanation.

Rumours swirled. One said that a band member was in urgent need of medical attention following excessive drug use, another claimed that Robert was unhappy considering himself redundant at the live show and more reasonably, that they just needed more time to rehearse the new material. Fans would have laughed off rumours like these in the past but after a three-year wait, tolerating another summer watching yet more upstarts make a claim to a crown they virtually invented would test their patience to the full.

When Primal Scream's first UK tour in three years finally commenced in Glasgow, a crazed member of the audience assaulted up to fourteen people by stabbing them with a hypodermic needle. Things were going from bad to worse. The band issued the following statement: "We are all collectively shocked and disturbed by this sick, degraded behaviour and our thoughts are with the people who were hurt and their families. We are frustrated and annoyed that this happened at a hometown gig which, for us and our fans, should have been a time of celebration and that these people, who had gone out purely to enjoy themselves, ended up getting injured by one stupid, irresponsible idiot." They urged all who were stabbed, and those who suspect they may have been, to quickly seek medical attention. Luckily, considering the nature of the attack, no serious consequences were reported.

Unbelievably, the remaining dates were postponed for a second time when it was learned that there would be no security at the London shows. The reason for this was the apparent necessity of the city's forces having to solely concern themselves with the prelude to the funeral of Diana Spencer, the Princess Of Wales who had recently died in a car accident. Promoters pulled the licence and for logistical and economic reasons were not able to rearrange just the shows in the capital.

The band were furious; they reacted angrily with a statement which read: "We have no respect whatsoever for Diana Spencer or any member of the English Royal Family. We are totally opposed to the monarchy. With regard to the London shows, the police refused to police the event, which meant the council would revoke the licence. We wanted to play."

To reinforce the point, when a recent performance of 'Star' on *TFI Friday* was repeated as part of a special tribute compilation in honour of the Princess, they once again made public their total lack of concern for all things royal.

Musically, the dates in general, on through Manchester, Wolverhampton and notably Victoria Park in London were unsatisfactory. And massively.

Standing in the crush by the stage, fans wearing *Give Out ...* T-shirts longed for the house lights to go down, a lank-haired band to swagger on and launch confidently into 'Jailbird' or 'Movin' On Up'. What they saw instead were five nervous looking men and their brass section slowly taking to their positions and standing motionless. The distant thunder of 'Burning Wheel' was barely recognisable as it leaked from the PA, while the shadowy figure of Bobby Gillespie stood droopily rooted to his mic stand. Projected onto the wall behind them were flickering black and white images of destruction, war and propaganda.

As the thick beat of 'Burning Wheel' kicked in following Robert's driving introduction, the shoving down the front intensified as young people - some of them no more than thirteen - began to spring around; finally making an example of the fact that they could identify the song after all and, for a brief and glorious moment, it seemed that despite the delays, the new Primal Scream were about to match the old. Robert and Mani looked healthy enough but Bobby and Andrew appeared stiff and overtly conscious of their responsibilities as entertainers. Before the end of the first song in Glasgow and Manchester dozens of kids were carried from the wedge of bodies, as the vibe in the crowds changed markedly from enthusiastic anticipation to protection of personal safety.

The second song, usually 'If They Move, Kill 'Em', petered away before 'Rocks' injected some much needed guile into the set, during which it became sadly apparent that something pretty essential was missing: coherence. The stomping beat sounded lifeless; it was provided not by human hand but technology that lacked the necessary timing, as their live instruments were unable to keep pace with the programmed loops.

As the set sluggishly crawled through much of the callow *Vanishing Point*, it was clear that the excitement and unpredictability expected of the night had already been found in their support act, the talented Asian Dub Foundation.

Professionally, as Primal Scream would later admit, the shows were a complete mess and with wounded pride they closed up as the press crucified them for sloppiness.

In the broad scheme of things, it didn't help Primal Scream that certain newer acts were dominating the hip market as Britpop was began to fade. The scruffy but brainy Radiohead were raging with their brand of angst-ridden psychedelic rock and The Verve, themselves having recently found importance of 'Loaded' like proportions, riding high with sample-stealing pop numbers and an effortlessly cool grasp of guitar melody. If Primal Scream were undisputed critical and commercial darlings in post-acid house Britain, then little more than half a decade later things were different and much bigger. Such a period of time can be an eternity in pop and even with the splendid return to form that was *Vanishing Point*, the shaky live performances confirmed that there was still much ground to be made up if they were to regain their status as the true band of the moment.

To many it's difficult to overstate the impact of dance culture on Primal Scream. Though morally a rock 'n' roll band in the finest tradition, their reinvention at the start of the 90s makes their story all the more fascinating.

If they hadn't come across Andy Weatherall, it has to be said, the chances are that they would probably have permanently stalled as a leather-garbed loser band stuck in yesteryear and they had been fully aware of the likelihood of that possibility. Their desperation, as it were, to escape to stardom saw them try anything; even the trendy fad that was dance music. With 'Loaded', they effectively compromised their beliefs, something they said they would never do, and as a result they became stars.

Inevitably, alternative mixes of their songs became commonplace following that first experiment, all of which continued to flourish in dance arenas. By early 1997 they'd even commissioned a whole album's worth of remixes from *Vanishing Point*. It was titled *Echo Dek*, a creation of Adrian Sherwood.

Sherwood had been just about Britain's busiest and most influential reggae producer. In his early twenties he launched numerous short-lived labels with a preference towards intricately mixed live recordings. While he saw little in the way of commercial success, his dub-inspired mixing techniques as On-U-Sound were such that major names from the world of synth-pop came calling; furthering his repertoire to dance and finally conventional rock.

"I'd heard about Adrian Sherwood," Bobby recalls, "and for some reason I thought he was going to be a really evil guy, a paranoid anarchist or something. I don't know why.." They'd first encountered each other back at Southern Studios when Bobby was recording with The Mary Chain, and as Primal Scream's reputation was in the ascendant, it was perhaps destiny that their paths would cross. Adrian first produced them for the Irvine Welsh football single and they were so impressed with the results that they offered him the remix LP in addition to the sound desk at recent live dates. Adrian was delighted to accept.

He reworked the tapes of *Vanishing Point* and came up with 'Living Dub', 'Duffed Up', 'Revolutionary', 'JU-87', 'First Name Unknown', 'Vanishing Dub', 'Last Train', 'Wise Blood' and 'Dub In Vain'. Splattered with cold dub sounds, *Echo Dek* was revolutionary; Primal Scream were still pushing the envelope, working with different people and exploring new music. Though the band's involvement with the composing of it had been minimal, it was yet more proof that they would stop at nothing to avoid being labelled a conventional band.

Bobby said at the time: "We're doing something that nobody else is. I mean, *Echo Dek* isn't some sort of rip-off record, it's a totally separate album that stands on its own. It's really dark and soulful, it's really beautiful." *Melody Maker* likewise wrapped up an ecstatic review by declaring: "Adrian Sherwood opens them up, creates space and melts more of the essence of Studio One greatness into the cracks than the tartan boys have ever sniffed at. Not simply a companion album, but every last inch of it is a brilliant creation in its own right."

Over at the supposedly more mature *Q*, thumbs were equally up: "You've got to admire their conviction," began Andrew Collins, "three months after the quite good indeed *Vanishing Point*, Primal Scream unleash the feature-length dub version. Proof that there is value in taking rock to its vanishing point." Spoiling the party, the *NME,* back-pedalling on the nine-out-of-ten given to *Vanishing Point*, called *Echo Dek* "pointless" and awarded an average six. Indeed, there was plenty of evidence to see the record both ways, as *Vanishing Point* was the album, remember, while *Echo Dek* was only the companion, but since the good reviews far outnumbered the bad, it could be looked back on as a successful experiment, with its fairly modest sales nothing but a bonus courtesy of diehard fans.

Vanishing Point, meanwhile, had been nominated for the Mercury Music Prize and if not for fine albums by Reprazent and The Charlatans would have surely been regarded as the finest long player of the year, while a third Oasis album, which Alan McGee predicted would sell twenty million, never sold half that amount and was eventually met with critical indifference. By then it was clear that Primal Scream had survived yet another musical craze and were still making some of the most exciting music around.

Shortly after the disappointing summer dates, and with their collective tails between their legs, the band ran off to Australia and the Far East where they first played with drummer Darrin Mooney. The set list was rearranged and with a human drummer the performances improved immeasurably. The poor shows in Britain had badly wounded their pride, as for all their talk about how they were going to be amazing, they'd actually been anticlimactic. Not only had their big comeback tour been twice delayed but when it finally arrived, they flopped, miserably and that would never do.

Not that they used the performances out there as mere rehearsals for a possible second British outing, far from it, but they wanted to be sharp when the inevitable was announced. In mid-February, they launched another attack on Britain's concert theatres. To seize the moment, Creation put out on limited release a wild and lengthy remix of 'If They Move, Kill 'Em' by former My Bloody Valentine mainman Kevin Shields, who had found an outlet for his undoubted talent that Primal Scream were quick to offer.

Kevin was a reclusive, lazy would-be perfectionist; a carefree studio maestro with a shocking disregard for conventional business discipline. Responsible for producing MBV's *Loveless* album, that had financially crippled Creation until Sony and Oasis came along, he was added to Primal Scream's ever-expanding production roster before someone else likely got him. Ever partial to the odd gamble, the band took the chance and in time it proved worth it. The more immediate matter however, was to get back on the road and prove to their loyal British fans that they could still cut it on stage.

The very accessibility of Primal Scream had always been one of the reasons that they appealed to young people looking for entertainment. Pleasingly, ticket prices were never too expensive and venues were never too large that they appeared impersonal or too small to seem insignificant. The places that they played were nearly always all-standing venues in urban areas, uniting both the working class youngsters looking for a night out and the denim-covered post-graduate types who'd followed their career for years. The forthcoming shows were essentially a fine example of what they did for a living. Tickets priced at twelve pounds were seen changing hands outside venues for five times their face value.

Discussing the tour, Bobby eagerly told *Vox*: "We've really tightened up since we played that Victoria Park gig. Really, it's a completely different band from four years ago, so it took a while for things to start sounding good. We wanted to marry the live thing with the technology and that took time but now that it's come together, now we've got a drummer, Mooney, who's the bedrock of the live shows, it's cool."

Indeed, the disappointing summer dates were now but a memory as *Vanishing Point* was brought crackling to life almost in its entirety. Opening the set with the intense combination of 'Out Of The Void' and 'Stuka', the fine concert promised from the record was fully delivered as an ambitious band tore through their songs, playing with all the invention of *Screamadelica* and the musicianship of *Give Out But Don't Give Up*.

The fun was enhanced by quirky performances of oldies like 'Imperial', 'Come Together' and even The Jesus And Mary Chain's 'Darklands'. The shows ended with a rousing version of MC5's 'Kick Out The Jams', a celebratory anthem that would be part of the set for the foreseeable future. It was obvious to all that they were enjoying themselves once again, unlike the statues that had fretted their way through the summer sets; Bobby's maraca shaking, in particular, was a sight to behold.

At Glasgow's Barrowlands, *Melody Maker's* Tony Naylor declared: "It's a stunning victory. And, improbable as it might sound, you sense that they're going to get better." BBC Radio One were given permission to record the concert and duly broadcast highlights of it later in the week.

Bobby: "I'm really into the idea of the whole spectacle of a gig and not just the main band, so I was pleased that we could get a great support band like Alabama 3. I loved their album, so we got them to play."

Alabama 3 were plucked from relative obscurity to warm up the crowd, something which they achieved with great success, regardless of the fact that the musical differences between them and their headliners were colossal. The concerts proved transparently levitating - sweltering entertainment in the mists of a bitterly cold winter.

Appearances at festivals across Europe and small shows in South America saw them in equally top form, and there was a feeling that a ghost had been laid over whether or not the album could actually be performed live. At the beginning of May any doubts were sublimely put to rest by an absolutely spectacular performance at the Creamfields festival. Although it was the inaugural conversion from Liverpool's top dance club Cream, it was perhaps Primal Scream's finest rock performance since Glastonbury back in '92. At the indoor Muzik Arena 'Burning Wheel' was truly hypnotic, while 'Rocks', starring Darrin Mooney, was simply note perfect. "We knew we'd done it," Bobby impassively told MTV, "we ripped it to bits..." The press agreed with a gushing air of vindication.

At Barrowlands again - their traditional hometown venue and the location of many a fine show - another storming night finally saw everything perfected for the band who'd set such high standards for themselves. A fleeting Jesus And Mary Chain provided the support, completing the circle started on 11 October 1984. It was a completely isolated show, captured on the bootleg *Kill All Hippies*, which was named after a line of dialogue they'd been using from the film *Out Of The Blue* prior to 'I'm Five Years Ahead Of My Time'. The riotous number was originally recorded by little known 60s outfit The Third Bardo and was widely expected to appear on the next long player.

But for the promotional visit a year earlier, America didn't see Primal Scream with *Vanishing Point*. For most of the era their new American label Reprise seemed unwilling or unable to provide the necessary support for a tour but on the whole it had been a successful period.

Concern now centred on whether the current momentum would last. Primal Scream were now older, seemingly more responsible and not championing older music so much. Some of the older music which they had always revered however was that of The Faces and, flatteringly, Rod Stewart himself had worked up his own complimentary version of 'Rocks' for his album *When We Were The New Boys*.

"It was an honour," said Bobby, "we're all big Faces fans. We love Ronnie Wood and Rod Stewart. I thought it was a great version because that song was pretty much inspired by The Faces and The Stones in the first place, so when Rod covered it, I thought it was fantastic."

Primal Scream scattered, with the loose intention of regrouping later in the year to record new songs that had apparently been written on the road. Bobby visited the Americas, while Andrew and Martin were spotted watching Scotland at the football World Cup Finals in France. Like a true Scotsman, Andrew was probably not too disappointed when his beloved country yet again failed to progress beyond the first round.

In 1998 The Jesus And Mary Chain disbanded. In the mid 80s, having signed to a major label and released an album that *Melody Maker* readers have since voted as the greatest of the decade, it looked as though they were the oft-heralded saviours of accessible rock. To many, it has been downhill ever since.

They were revolutionary; two brothers who dared to combine polar opposite sounds in an era when neither was remotely fashionable. That they managed to pull it off was in no small way due to the help of Alan McGee and Bobby Gillespie, two young men who used the Reid brothers to headbutt their way into the business.

Alan knew that any publicity was good publicity, and when The Mary Chain came along he grabbed his chance with both hands. McGee concocted an image of his find that was hardly an accurate reflection of them either as musicians or people. The riots, the bans, the controversy; while great for Alan's ego and the profile of Creation, reflected badly on Jim and William Reid, who soon found themselves lumped with a reputation that limited their every move.

In 1986 they sacked Alan as their manager and as predicted the publicity soon dried up but they were able to flourish as talented musicians. The four albums they had made since *Psychocandy* saw melodies take prominence over noise and acclaim rightly flooded in. Though they were commercially overtaken by Primal Scream, relations remained good and, shortly before the split they were welcomed back to Creation by Alan, who was longing for a return of some of the old camaraderie.

Jim and William had a sixth album titled *Munki* in the can and presented it to Alan, who put it out to critical acclaim, if not huge sales. No sooner had Bobby provided them with backing vocals at one of their subsequent shows he caught in California, when the differences that had been obvious from the very dawn of The Mary Chain came to a spectacular head on stage. It was perhaps just another case of sibling rivalry, but the brothers parted acrimoniously and went their seperate professional ways.

The band that put Creation Records on the map was finally gone forever.

xtrmntr

Satpal Ram's supporters claim he was minding his own business; he was eating in the Birmingham restaurant in 1986 when a group of racist hooligans attacked him, stabbing him in the face with broken glass. In self-defence, Satpal used a small knife he carried for work purposes and fought off one of his assailants. Both men were cut and taken to hospital where Ram's attacker refused treatment and later died. The prosecution's claim - that Ram was a drunken abusive thug, carrying an illegal knife and looking to use his ethnicity as motivation if slighted - saw him convicted of murder and sentenced to life. Primal Scream aligned themselves with his defence. Along with Asian Dub Foundation they performed a concert in March '98 that was said to have raised more than fifty thousand pounds for Ram's freedom campaign. Bobby campaigned especially hard for his release, even visiting him in prison to offer support.

Performers using their influence to make people aware of what they consider injustices was certainly nothing new. Five albums into their turbulent career, it seemed as though Bobby Gillespie had finally realised that if he was actually going to sing something mature, then it may as well be about what was on his mind, be it radio friendly or not. Always politically conscious, by his late thirties Bobby had seen a lot of the world and saw no reason not to speak out.

"In the past, I was always quite self-conscious as a lyricist and I found it difficult to write but I've become more confident," he said, "I'm writing about the culture and what we see and what's going down. Even if we haven't written about certain topics, I'm sure that if you engaged us in conversation anytime since we were about sixteen we were always contentious and questioning things." Whatever the case, it was a far cry from the pleasure seeking scarecrow that had fronted Primal Scream for all those years previously.

Suddenly, everything was very serious.

In the UK there would no doubt be a couple of hundred thousand people who would buy a new Primal Scream album regardless of the lyrics but whether the more conscious sections of their fanclub would understand their message and - more importantly, acknowledge it - was a dilemma that could potentially cause the band bad press and consequently decrease sales. Many younger bands in Britain were now selling considerably more records than Primal Scream ever had, saying safe, bland and quite untrue things that no doubt helped their marketable image tenfold. Lightweight singalongs were suddenly the flavour of the moment, as if the industry was making a desperate attempt to regain lost sales in the wake of a late 90s multimedia explosion. Primal Scream hated the blandness that ruled the airwaves, they hated how it was neither here nor there, as Mani astutely pointed out to an American journalist: "It would be easy to be careerist and just play a lot of rubbish and get paid heaps of money like a lot of people do but that's not what we're about at all. I'd rather starve for the integrity of knowing we tried something different."

Not long after being feted by Primal Scream in the mid 90s, The Dust Brothers changed their name to The Chemical Brothers for legal reasons and had since topped both singles and album charts. Ed Simons and Tom Rowlands had become a blown-up equivalent of the act that Primal Scream had once been and with the rivalry remaining friendly, both groups were keen to continue collaborating. Along with New Order's Bernard Sumner, Bobby appeared on The Brothers' excellent 'Out Of Control' which became a hit single and was included in the much fussed over film *The Beach*.

Again, and only slightly less prestigious was Bobby's contribution to Death In Vegas' highly arresting 'Soul Auctioneer'. Having the face of Primal Scream guest on one's music was now of significant promotional value, but still, since Bobby considered the songs good enough he was delighted to be asked to work with people of integrity. Death In Vegas would now join a list with the likes of The Orb, Kris Needs, The Sabres Of Paradise, Asian Dub Foundation and Alabama 3 who all gained a higher profile following stints either opening for Primal Scream or recording with them. By the final year of the twentieth century Primal Scream were seen as survivors and considered key; suspicions that their next album would confirm.

By early '99 the band had quickly written and recorded the best part of the most hard-hitting album of their career. Much of the following year was then given over to post-production. Finding the right people to try their hand with the tapes led to no shortage of offers, not least from Kevin Shields, who the *NME* perhaps erroneously reported had fully joined the band. His remix of 'If They Move, Kill 'Em', subtitled 'MBV Arkestra', had been a huge critical success which furthered his involvement in the studio and would also see him added to the live ranks.

Premiered on the last tour, the take of The Third

Bardo's 'I'm Five Years Ahead Of My Time' included actress Linda Manz's voice from the movie *Out Of The Blue*, as she ordered: "Destroy and kill all hippies." The dialogue was transported to a new home, a namesake track that would begin the album. 'Kill All Hippies' evolved into a funky bass-driven number with building space noises and a falsetto vocal. 'I'm Five Years Ahead Of My Time' meanwhile was losing ground amongst the glut of new material, as was 'Sick City', a Stoogesesque insurrection cut with David Holmes, Northern Ireland's mix superstar.

Having been impressed by the music Holmes had written for a vodka advertisement, he was approached to work on the jazz punk 'Blood Money' and the almost unbearably bleak 'Keep Your Dreams'. Talking about Primal Scream, Holmes declared: "It's amazing working with them. There aren't many bands like Primal Scream around any more. There's too many bands playing it safe. The Scream wear their hearts on their sleeve. They've zero tolerance for anything negative." Undoubtedly, such compliments would never have been made of Primal Scream pre 'Loaded', proving that whatever the knockers said about their propensity to have DJs, producers and fellow musicians mix them, such an opportunity was now simply one of the most sought after CV references in contemporary British music. The band's resistance to allowing their egos anywhere near the mixing desk could only be applauded.

There remained room for several old friends, those being Hugo Nicholson, Adrian Sherwood and Brendan Lynch to contribute to the new songs, one of which was the amazing 'Shoot Speed/Kill Light'. With its screaming looped guitar, highly reminiscent of Joy Division, it seemed only appropriate that it should feature Bernard Sumner recreating the part. The ex-Joy Division guitarist's contribution helped ensure that 'Shoot Speed...' would be one of the most intense songs on the record and a perfect last track. Bobby's long-held promise that Primal Scream would make an album that was raw, uncompromising and deeply claustrophobic would soon be delivered.

It was The Chemical Brothers though, who oversaw their first single since 'If They Move, Kill 'Em' almost two years before. 'Swastika Eyes' was a shocking, offensive disco mantra that sounded as though it had been constructed entirely from technology. Lyrically, it was a bitter and confrontational insult to authority, the like of which even this chameleon singer had never before delivered.

"'Swastika Eyes' is about the new world order, American international terrorism," Bobby told *Jockey*

Slut, "it's about control. It's a great image, a great insult: 'You've got swastika eyes' - it applies to any authoritarian figure; a politician or a policeman - you see them everywhere."

Not surprisingly it caused controversy at radio stations everywhere, with even the bravest awarding it only minimal exposure. The fluff was sidestepped wherever possible, some international labels renaming it 'War Pigs'. Jagz Kooner also reworked 'Swastika Eyes' into a turbo-charged seven-minute extravaganza. Including two mixes of the same track on the album signified how much attention they wanted on the title, recalling The Sex Pistols scoring an unofficial number one with 'God Save The Queen', when publicity claimed that their record sleeve almost featured a Queen Elizabeth portrait with swastikas over her eyes. Unsurprisingly the single wasn't a chart success.

The promotional film to accompany the Chemical Brothers mix was largely overlooked, likely considered too experimental even for the medium of music video. Not helped by the rapid fire editing; when comprehensible, it featured a military camouflaged Primal Scream watching what appears to be a rural fashion show, with supermodel Sophie Dahl offensively pouting in the chaos. The British release saw three mixes on the CD format, the countless beats-per-minute Chemical Brothers take, the likewise Jagz Kooner cut and a lesser combination of the two. Nobody could have seriously expected the ambiguously labelled release to do especially well, but its entry and peak position of number twenty-two could have been much worse in the pre-Christmas market. The two main mixes regularly turned up on British television in the forthcoming months, notably the Chemical Brothers version that accompanied credits of Sky Television's coverage of the Nationwide Football League.

In late 1999 with the album complete and awaiting release, Alan McGee announced his decision to terminate Creation Records with immediate effect. In the previous sixteen years Alan had seen his ambitions go from cheaply pressed singles by bands featuring his best friends, to a coveted role on a Government committee intended to benefit Britain's pressing cultural matters. In between he'd provided the world with a fifteen million selling album by Britain's biggest pop phenomenon since The Beatles. His reasons for closing Creation have, for many, never been made clear but in several interviews prior to his shock announcement Alan hinted that the availability of music over the internet would further cripple record labels and for brave independents would prove the final straw.

It hurt but having made the decision Alan told *Select*: "Truthfully, I don't think I'll miss anything. If I fell out with Bobby, I'd miss that but if I've got my friendships then I've got enough. I'll keep in touch with the people who are my friends here but I need a new start."

McGee was set for life; approaching forty he had unquestionably left a positive mark on British indie music but in the end felt things at his label had gone too far in the wrong direction, it was now too comfortable and many of his recent staff were seemingly unable to acknowledge just how far the business had come. He elaborated: "I think pre-Sony was the best musical time for Creation, that period from '84 to '93. I mean, double respect to Oasis, but what was going on in the company then was amazing. We were just totally out of control. And through the madness came a lot of good records."

Quite naturally, as Alan now admits, once everything got comfortable, Creation became complacent. Little more than five years previously it was inconceivable that the biggest band on the label wouldn't be Primal Scream, so when it became clear that Oasis were, beyond any reasonable doubt, not just kings of the castle but the whole solar system, for the secure, hard working mainstay that was Bobby's band, there simply must have been some envy, privately at the very least.

Suddenly, from being able to enjoy the often exciting uncertainty of the brave label's future, they saw it become the glitzy toast of the industry; everything that Alan and Bobby had despised for all those years. To his credit, Alan was alert enough to acknowledge this but one suspects that it certainly wasn't before Primal Scream, in one way or another, made it clear to him that morally, Creation Records was dead and buried.

From the outset Creation had been an alternative record company which existed for nine whole years without any kind of solid backing from a major. During that time it was more often than not in debt, surviving from hand to mouth on a minute budget and a ton of enthusiasm. For the label to have gotten as far as it did without having played the corporate game deserves heartfelt praise indeed but the fact that its very achievements were brashly flaunted often left the impression that even million-selling albums was never quite enough. That, however, was before Oasis terrorised the world, which for Alan, must have been the ultimate case of 'be careful what you wish for'.

Without his friendship with Alan McGee, Bobby Gillespie's musical efforts might have been limited to little more than karaoke rants. He would certainly have made music, that was obvious to anyone who'd ever heard him rave about his favourite records with a passion unmatched in contemporary music but the fact remains that Primal Scream had essentially benefited from Alan's hard work, desire and sheer luck. Since Oasis albums had sold in their millions, everything recent on the label was financed without the worries of before, ultimately meaning that with *Vanishing Point* Primal Scream had been freeloaders.

Now, one might argue that because of Bobby, Alan found The Jesus And Mary Chain, the band that put Creation on the map and made him believe that it really could be done. Or, perhaps it was Andrew Innes's headlong dive into drug-infested clubland that eventually inspired *Screamadelica*, the success of which was instrumental in keeping the label afloat.

"If we hadn't met Andy Weatherall and we hadn't have made 'Loaded', then Creation wouldn't have got bigger and they would never have signed Oasis. It's a weird one," elaborated Bobby, "lots of things would never have happened." Perhaps Alan and Bobby's contributions to each other's careers added up equal but from the beginning, for Gillespie, a music obsessive looking for an outlet to expressive himself, having a close friend run a liberal record label was maybe just too convenient.

Six months after Creation's closure, Bobby was relaxed enough about the whole issue to declare: "I saw it coming for a long time and I was pleased that it happened because it had become something that it had set out to destroy and it needed to be destroyed itself. There was no reason for its existence. I respect Alan because he wasn't enjoying it. He needs a challenge and he's happy now. He's free of Sony. The big corporations, these people, they buy a part of you, end up owning you and you're finished."

On Creation, in industry terms, Primal Scream had got away with absolute murder and gained a rather maverick reputation for their unpredictability. Now, no mistake should be made about a matter which suddenly had immediate relevance: conventional record companies, especially those like Creation's parent Sony, just don't accommodate maverick behaviour. Not at all.

The cocktail of *Vanishing Point* encapsulated Primal Scream's sound in one album and few could have predicted how they would return. In retrospect, it was the calm before the storm. The recent war imagery, like the flying Stuka plane and the war footage that backdropped live performances, was perhaps the first hint of their future intent. The attitude from *Vanishing*

Point remained, it had just strengthened, was more focused and even less welcoming.

Bobby: "I don't hear strong individual voices any more. Too many cowards, too many people with no imagination. There's no insurrection or call to arms in any records except ours these days. No one's writing 'Get Up Stand Up', they're all writing songs for adverts. I think the new album is really pure, it's direct and brutal. It tells it like it is or how we see it."

Noticeably, the singer mentioned that the undeniable discontent implied by the new album was how they saw Britain, even if no one else saw it like that. He was quick to add that for all their apparent anger, Primal Scream were not preaching to anyone, but encouraging people to think for themselves; their music was, after all, just stimulating and thought provoking entertainment...

Omitting vowels on puzzling grounds of apparent fascism, the album was titled *Xtrmntr*, (Exterminator) and released as the last ever Creation album in January 2000. The UK version contained 'Kill All Hippies', 'Accelerator', 'Exterminator', 'Swastika Eyes (Jagz Kooner mix)', 'Pills', 'Blood Money', 'Keep Your Dreams', 'Insect Royalty', 'If They Move, Kill 'Em (MBV Arkestra)', 'Swastika Eyes (Chemical Brothers mix)', and 'Shoot Speed/Kill Light'.

If, to be ultra-critical, the remixes ensured that a quarter of the album wasn't new material, little did it matter as *Xtrmntr* provided Primal Scream with not only some of the best reviews of their career but arguably as spectacular a critical response to any cutting edge record Britain had seen since Britpop.

Q declared: "even when you're listening to it with your hands over your ears, anyone with the first notion about rock 'n' roll will catch the whiff of authentic mayhem here." *Muse* added: "how a group of messed up posturing desperados have managed to make a record that sounds so completely and utterly now we don't quite know." "*Xtrmntr* is exactly the shot in the arm that rock needs right now," the astute *Dot Music* observed, "it's the antithesis of the elements that shaped the redundant vortex of 1999's music scene." The *NME*, before awarding nine-out-of-ten said: "if it had a colour, *Xtrmntr* would be blinding white." Album of the Month accolades were awarded by *Select*, *Uncut*, *FHM* and *Sky*; the usually exclusively dance mag *Mixmag* awarded full marks, while weekly prizes even came in from the normally subdued broadsheets like *The Guardian* and *The Daily Telegraph*. If you were in Primal Scream, it was a good time to read your own press.

As pointed out in many of the reviews, in

conventional terms the album was a god-awful racket; in particular the aptly titled 'Accelerator' was surely one of the most over the top and uncontrolled ear-splitting spectaculars ever committed to vinyl. The rap-like offence of the filth strewn 'Pills' was as harrowing as one could imagine and the new take of 'Insect Royalty' smelled of urban rot. The multi-layered instruments and studio technology were mixed at such volume that the sounds could hardly be described as 'music', as traditional melody was only scarcely present. The term 'disco-punk' was invented, which almost did the record justice, but unless they could fully detach themselves from old accusations of Rolling Stones plagiarism and attract part of, say, the ferociously developing 'Nu Metal' audience, Primal Scream could hardly complain if such a blatantly un-commercial record didn't sell in its millions. The album entered the charts at number three but made no further progress. They were already on the road, as they would remain for much of the year.

With Kevin Shields on third guitar and Jim Hunt and Duncan Mackay on horns, the nine-man outfit had set off on a tour that would prove to be the band's largest jaunt for six years. Unlike the *Give Out...* haul, the *Xtrmntr* dates would be more spacious, in an attempt to ensure that fatigue would be less of a factor, as they wanted to perform as enthusiastically for audiences at the end of the tour as to those at the start.

Beginning in Asia, then on to Britain, America and mainland Europe by the end of spring, the *Xtrmntr* tour wouldn't end until New Year's Eve in London, climaxing a hastily arranged second British trip of the year just prior to Christmas. For Bobby's sixteen-year-old band, the performances were spectacular. Contrary to some post *Vanishing Point* claims that they were 'always rubbish' at the start of a tour, as certainly by the multi-date 'Big Day Out' festival down under, Primal Scream were, strictly in disco punk terms, absolutely scorching.

On stage Robert was as pretty as ever, while Mani would yell at the audience and always give the impression that he was loving the moment. Bobby would frequently look emotionless as he cried into his microphone, wrapped in a thick military shirt and oversized mirror sunglasses. Kevin Shields was a more anonymous sight, strumming casually next to the spirited figure of Andrew Innes. On the back line, barely visible under stacks of keys, sat Martin Duffy, on hand to provide the sampled noises and traditional piano solos as of years gone by. Next to the horns double act was drummer Darrin Mooney, pounding out the beat of a concert that wasn't to be missed.

With a video animating the album artwork, 'Kill All Hippies' was released as a single to coincide with more than a dozen dates around Britain during March and April, all of them in three to five thousand capacity venues. A throw back to the *Screamadelica* tour, the dates would see the band hit the stage late, usually around half past eleven, and play through until after one. At various stages the supporting cast included David Holmes and Death In Vegas but there was to be no show stealing, as night after night Primal Scream's assault on the ears was a riotous masterpiece of disco rock rhythms. While the set was mostly made up from the new album, *Vanishing Point* was represented by 'Burning Wheel', 'Kowalski', 'If They Move, Kill 'Em' and 'Medication', *Give Out...* provided only 'Rocks', whilst *Screamadelica* offered 'Movin' On Up' and 'Higher Than The Sun'. Like last time the show ended with a roof-raising 'Kick Out The Jams'.

The audiences, fully stirred up by the excitement of the show, were pleasingly proactive but on more than one occasion a little too much so. At The Ritz in Manchester, just before the penultimate song 'Movin' On Up', a container filled with drink was slung on stage, nearly soaking stacks of equipment - an electrifying band were quickly threatened with electrocution.

Bobby paused to lecture the heckler, before discovering that his microphone had failed after Andrew had begun the next song. "I was blind, now I can see, you made a believer, out of me, I'm movin' on up now!" sang the audience, before Bobby was able to continue with an otherwise perfect delivery of the old favourite.

By April, after two nights in Glasgow and one at The Royal Court in Liverpool, Bobby and the whole band walked off stage at the Town and Country in Leeds, having almost been hit for the second time by a missile. After a few moments of confused shouting above a rumbling undertone of genuine concern, they returned, much to everyone's relief, seemingly unaffected before powering through their intended set.

Two dates later at the Brighton Centre, the *NME* was emphatically thrilled to witness such an occasion; calling them the best live band on the planet. Visiting London's stages for the second time, there were two sold out nights at the Brixton Academy and an isolated date after a spin round Europe in the first week of May, at the Shepherd's Bush Empire, filmed for broadcast by MTV for their *Five Night Stand* series.

For America, after being dropped by Reprise, the recognised dance label Astralwerks took on the album, with an option to pick them up on a longer term basis dependent on its success. Before the label released the album in May, Primal Scream had already agreed to cross the pond and put the work in. With the support of the influential college radio networks eleven dates were booked in venues with an average capacity of fifteen hundred. Executed in a smart zig-zag from 26 May in Washington DC, the tour took in Boston, New York, Toronto and Detroit until June, then down through Chicago, Dallas, Austin and Denver; their first American tour since the infamous Depeche Mode dates would end in California with shows in Los Angeles and San Francisco.

After a satisfactory first show, the second date was at the Boston WBCN Radio Festival where, as is quite normal for breaking 'alternative' acts, much of the day before the show was given over to public relations announcing their arrival. There was nothing unusual in Bobby doing lots of interviews for an album but this time, from reading what he said, he seemed far more dismissive than ever before - he seemed to be permanently angered by everything and anything. Pouring forth swear words, he and Mani would launch into their polished double act of ferociously criticising everything from the British Government to the apparent state of most of their musical contemporaries. Journalists often found it difficult to get a question in edgeways, being too busy trying to make coherent sense of the rants they were subjected to. While no one's saying that the pair weren't entitled to their opinion, or that they weren't even correct, it did get tiring for fans to read the same four quotes in every interview. As personalities, they were in danger of becoming an earache nobody wanted.

Reviewing the show at New York's Hammerstein Ballroom, the *NME's* correspondent raved: "We Yanks turn to the motherland for true rock stars and, let's face it, Gillespie is one of the last. The raucous capacity crowd tonight not only know it but embrace their hero. He shows New York City that he has finally abandoned his heroes and come into his own, leading us through a discovery of electronic punk for the twenty-first century." Almost all the shows in America had sold out where the set, save for the premiere of 'Sick City', had barely changed from what they'd been playing all year.

At the House Of Blues in Los Angeles, they were joined by Sex Pistol Steve Jones on guitar for triumphant covers of The Stooges' 'No Fun' and the usual 'Kick Out The Jams'. Filmed for a multimedia broadcast, some footage was cut with riot scenery to illustrate 'Accelerator'. The provocative nature of the video, produced by Douglas Hart and Grant Fleming, was again seemingly too extreme to fully promote the imminent single, the last-ever Creation Record.

Back in the UK there were the usual appearances at the annual Reading and Leeds festivals - of which the ailing *Melody Maker* was surprisingly critical - but still, the year had been going well and critically, following two modern, highly acclaimed releases, it seemed as if Primal Scream had finally escaped accusations of being karaoke rockers and found their true musical identity.

Xtrmntr had come out, sold steadily and regardless of whether its creators cared, was widely seen as the year's best album by the type of act that the *NME* felt belonged only to their readerships. So much had changed since the heyday of Britpop, not least because of the internet which had massively widened the choice and availability of entertainment coverage, hurting traditional industry methods as Alan had predicted. Almost twenty years previously McGee had been bursting with the punk spirit, photocopying his fanzine whereas his modern equivalent was glued to the omni-present home computer. It was more practical, of course, but through ever-increasing complacency, the working spirit so essential to rock 'n' roll was fading. Primal Scream, the old heads that they were, tried as best they could to cling to their post-punk roots. The anarchic but modern noise of *Xtrmntr* had been a fitting end to Creation and, like the first Jesus And Mary Chain record, proved that it could actually be done without production gloss or radio airplay. They had benefited by being the antithesis of what was considered popular music, while the overall concept of the people's band in general was now being restrained by an industry in a desperate and truly shameful state.

Looking around the album charts and thus picking up the general vibe, recent heavyweights were slowly but surely changing places with artificial acts; created by producers, television shows and record companies; no doubt acting in damage control mode to recover precious funds. Oasis were perhaps the most obvious example. Less than five years before they had epitomised the whole Britpop attitude as their music captivated the nation, yet they had matured in time to watch their own bubble burst.

Blur had proved flexible enough to retain some integrity before venturing on to solo projects and Pulp had gone on extended hiatus after a vast drop-off in sales. Radiohead had proved perhaps too ambitious after *OK Computer* and saw subsequent, more left-field work come and go overnight, while acts like The Verve and Sleeper had given up completely. The Union Jack that so proudly flew high during the mid 90s was now limping along at half-mast.

Just where Primal Scream stood in all this was a matter of opinion but while many of their supposed peers were struggling to keep up with their Britpop past, they just happened to be ferociously rebelling against everything; the main reason of course why the welcome and uncompromising *Xtrmntr* was so meaningful.

In retrospect, the inventor of the dreaded phrase 'Britpop' was more than likely a bigoted, English, London-based industry ego and hardly Primal Scream anyway. Much the world's forgotten boys at the time, once it had all blown over and helped by word of mouth and performances that blew the competition away, they became regarded as progressively more important.

Primal Scream; be they Brits, Scots, Celts or simply human beings, were surely the last great rock 'n' roll band around.

Earlier in the year, the band's financial advisor and accountant had been sacked, as a considerable amount of money had gone missing from their account. His firm was accused of using their funds to settle personal irregularities. For some months, manager

Alex Nightingale had been in trouble, unable to explain how this could have happened. He and Primal Scream parted ways in August.

Whatever Primal Scream had gone through in the past, these blemishes were really the first time in their history when signs of serious discontent leaked out. Despite their image as rebels, Bobby, Andrew and Robert always appeared united and organised, as Nightingale, in spite of a chequered past, had been a good manager, responsible on more than one occasion for motivating them to get out and do what they love. His dismissal surprised many, the details of which are likely to remain confidential, but it's assumed that the band were unhappy that he failed to look after their interests.

Without a manager, Bobby approached Alan to once again take over but he declined, only able to offer help on a part-time basis whilst he concentrated on his new label Poptones. To their eternal credit, Primal Scream didn't then disappear into legal hell but stuck together and accepted an inevitable offer from the promoters SJM Concerts to perform a short domestic tour just prior to Christmas.

Six dates were lined up, from the Cambridge Corn Exchange on 16 December, on through Brighton, Bristol, Birmingham and Manchester to The Point

Theatre in Dublin by December 23. On New Year's Eve at London's eight-thousand capacity Alexandra Palace they would headline 'Resolution 2000', supported by Asian Dub Foundation and Mani's old Roses mate Ian Brown.

The set was much the same as before, changing only with the inclusion of 'Sick City', the return of 'Loaded', and with the substitution of 'Keep Your Dreams' for *Vanishing Point's* 'Long Life'. Martin Duffy was absent from the stage, having recently broken a leg, but thanks to the wonders of technology his trademark piano lines were admirably present and audiences didn't seem to notice the join. The band themselves though couldn't have helped but notice some yawning empty spaces, as the half-empty venues confirmed the dangers of charging up to twenty pounds a ticket for shows the week before Christmas.

Still, the short and lucrative outing ended the year well, a year that, save for the financial difficulties, would have been largely perfect for Primal Scream. It was their live shows, first and foremost, which proved that they not only still existed but could teach the all-singing, all-dancing young pretenders just how per-suasive music could be. It was purity; war you could dance to.

As predicted, *Xtrmntr* **was duly** awarded the best album accolade at the *NME* awards and its showing was much the same in many other end of year polls. The huge critical success of the album and the substantial touring saw well over half a million units shifted which, although healthy for massively applauded veterans and cornerstones of the UK's elite, was certainly not heavy. All of Primal Scream's albums throughout the 90s had sold between half a million and a million copies, maintaining their success on a comfortable level, but there remained the feeling that they could have done better.

In an era of MTV creations and overnight multi-platinum successes, it was beginning to look as though Primal Scream would be doomed as an act known for good albums but relatively modest sales. Admittedly this was not the worst problem one could envisage but with labels less prepared to press albums that didn't fly off the shelves (by now copies of *Sonic Flower Groove* and *Primal Scream* were mostly found in second-hand stores) one couldn't help but wonder if they had already reached the top of their mountain.

Whether they would now be prepared to spend the rest of their career playing to the same audiences in the same venues as they had a decade previously was another question for the band. Always able to talk a good game, Bobby would repeatedly declare that they were stronger than ever; it was a secure cycle of self-promotion but it sometimes left him uncomfortable; looking back on occasions when things didn't quite turn out as planned.

Discussing, say, *Give Out But Don't Give Up* years after it came out, much like *Sonic Flower Groove,* Gillespie could hardly find a good word to say about it. He knew very well that the record isn't what his band would be remembered for, being far removed from the universally acclaimed LPs they'd made before and after.

It was 'a natural progression of ideas' is what he usually claimed but they argued that the changes were as a result of no particular talent in any particular genre. It was even claimed that *Vanishing Point* wasn't a step forward but a clever attempt via studio trickery to reclaim ground when its predecessor failed to weave its way inside the listener's consciousness. Like the record that Weatherall had made for them previously. The age old accusation was that Primal Scream basically had no spine, that they were a bunch of imposters cocooned by remixers, label bosses and large record collections; this criticism was hurtful and would seemingly never end.

If they were to disappear from public view, then now

would be precisely the right time for a hibernation and while that was largely the plan, 2001 would see the band active, and not always for the best of reasons.

With a General Election looming, it was reported that Primal Scream's 1992 hit single 'Movin' On Up' was considered by the campaigning Labour Party to be their election song. Following the championing of Labour leader Tony Blair four years previously by Oasis's Noel Gallagher and his and Alan's subsequent Downing Street day out, relations between the Government and what was left of the undoubtedly influential Creation family, staunchly left wing in origin, appeared to be in good health. To Primal Scream however, all the back slapping of the past four years hadn't been in the best interests of those who should benefit from a Labour Government. In fact, like much of the country, they claimed that their policies were more to the advantage of the middle classes. Bobby hinted that Primal Scream's music is not made for the pleasure of such people, while 'Movin' On Up', needless to say, did not promote any political party.

With Creation now defunct, Primal Scream were without an immediate home. Since 1985, even considering their brief, hardly successful liaison with Warner Brothers, they had very much been the house band of Alan McGee's label and every bit as important

as The Jesus And Mary Chain or Oasis. Rumours of
their demise had circulated frequently but they always
stuck together and made the music that only they
wanted. Now, without the support of Alan, who had
given them carte blanche at Creation, the next bout of
inevitable questions on their future were swiftly
countered by the assumption that they were now
employed by Sony, though no one, it seemed, could
get very specific on the matter. The fact that they
owned their own studio was encouraging, as they
could continue to record music, and by now it could be
safely assumed that what they produced would
always be at least interesting and worthy of useful
press.

Meanwhile, Alan was onto pastures new. His new
label Poptones seemed far removed from the glamour
of post-Oasis Creation and its founder made no secret
of his desire to reconnect with the roots that had first
inspired him all those years ago. Bobby, Robert and
Andrew, who'd been there since the very beginning,
soon came to terms with Alan's decision and its
consequences. Throughout the year they were spotted
indulging in Poptones sponsored club nights as well as
recording and appearing with a wide variety of
touring buddies.

Innes, predictably, found it nigh impossible to tear

himself away from the studio and Mani, understandably for someone who'd seen half a decade pass between albums in his last band, wasn't about to let the grass grow either. In 2000 he had played in a so-called supergroup called Mad For The Racket that had been put together by Wayne Kramer of MC5 and Brian James of The Damned. Also included in the ranks had been former Blondie member Clem Burke and The Police's Stewart Copeland. Mani recalls: "Duff McKagan [former Guns 'n' Roses bassist] is their normal man but he'd just had a kid. So Wayne Kramer was at one of Alan McGee's Poptones nights in London and Alan put him on to me. I got to play with bloody Wayne Kramer! You know our feelings about MC5, so it was amazing." Always up for a challenge, Mani was even making preparations to develop a career as a television presenter. He was lined up to present a couple of programmes called *Nu Music* for the cable channel UK Play. Yet just as all seemed well away from Primal Scream duty, this harmony was interrupted by a controversy involving the lead singer.

When Bobby appeared with J Mascis and The Fog at the Shepherd's Bush Empire that summer, it appeared that he crossed the line in a truly shocking and disgraceful manner. On stage for a version of 'No Fun', appropriately with former Stooge Ron Asheton present, Bobby wasn't much appreciated by certain Mascis fans in the front row. What happened then is a matter of conjecture, but to generalise widely circulated hearsay, after being thoroughly booed and showered with spit, Gillespie retaliated by forcefully smashing his microphone stand into an audience member before fleeing the building.

The talents of Bobby Gillespie will always be a topic of debate and his silence surrounding the alleged incident did him few favours, even with many diehard fans. From someone who was hardly a gifted vocalist, or anyone for that matter, the sheer irresponsibility of attacking an audience member swung public opinion closer to the conclusion that he was yet another talentless brat with no concept of reality.

Gillespie's public persona had often appeared contradictory, as one minute he seemed to be a talkative, enthusiastic bundle of grinning fun, the next a passively shy character and then an all together can't-be-bothered rock star far too wrapped up in his own perceived importance to acknowledge the people who put him where he was. Nobody, though, could claim to have anticipated the incident at the Empire, as by any stretch of the imagination his alleged actions were shockingly out of character.

His next press appearance was, thankfully, on a more positive note; thanks to New Order, returning the ball since Bernard Sumner's appearance on 'Shoot Speed/Kill Light'. Bobby and Andrew contributed to New Order's 'Rock The Shack', which contained a chord sequence imported from the Primal Scream song and was included on *Get Ready*, the Mancunians' first studio album in eight years.

As a big Joy Division fan, the opportunity to appear as a celebrity contributor to an eagerly-awaited New Order album must have helped Bobby realise just how far he'd come. Since New Order, the undisputed godfathers of independent integrity, had been dormant for almost a decade, Primal Scream, it appeared, were by now their only realistic contemporaries. Somehow, in the face of great adversity, they had outlasted most of their original, secondary and even third set of peers, in the process attaining the honourable status of respected elder statesmen. The difference between Primal Scream and many other middle-aged rockers, however, was that Bobby and company still made challenging music that was considered important. Age, it appeared, accelerated their work rate.

Amongst rumours of Bobby touring with New Order, Primal Scream regrouped to perform a handful of concerts after a break of more than eight months. Strutting on stage at London's intimate Astoria, they premiered three new songs, one provisionally titled 'Bomb The Pentagon'. The performance proved that they had lost none of their power as a live band, while the sell-out crowd were loudly enthusiastic throughout. Ever loyal to their army of Japanese fans, not for the first time they then took their show to sold out crowds at The Liquid Room in Tokyo where they performed the same set.

It was highly unusual for Primal Scream to play shows with no new material out and, in light of the terrorist attacks that occurred on September 11, 'Bomb The Pentagon' would prove a test for such a staunchly anti-Establishment band.

evil heat

The birth of Bobby's son was wonderful news and many considered that if this didn't force him to see the world in a different light, then perhaps he never would. By his fortieth year it was difficult for even the most inspired of prophets to speculate on where his band could go next as essentially, to all intents and purposes, they had done everything already.

Not that it stopped them trying. Mani, as ever doing his PR bit, was firing off encouraging vibes. He said of Primal Scream in 2002: "It's an exciting time to be in the Scream now because we know we've got a tremendous power that a lot of groups will never know. I think we've probably used the studio side of it a bit more than the live playing this time out; there's a lot of sequencing going on; we're forever trying to perfect how we make music and look for different ways we can utilise technology. I think we're intelligent enough to be able to do that."

Primal Scream had embraced technology to such an extent that, post-*Vanishing Point*, it appeared that the guitar, bass, drums outfit who had spent years learning their trade was unlikely to return anytime soon.

While first takes were often as genuinely rock 'n' roll as ever, *Evil Heat* was ultimately the sound of a studio band more creatively ambitious than just about anyone of their generation. Their eternal talk of togetherness no doubt included those on their list of producers that this time round included Kevin Shields, Jagz Kooner, Keith Tenniswood and the returning lord Andy Weatherall.

"It's like a production thing here," Bobby told *Digimusic*, "we're not bogged down by the standard band/musician rules, where everybody's ego has to be fulfilled. It'd be boring to have the same guys playing the same instruments on every song. It doesn't seem to work that well for us. We like to use different instruments for different sounds. We try and create atmospheres... and some of the sounds, you know, I don't know where they come from. Then we get the performances from people when we need them."

The track listing of *Evil Heat* was: 'Deep Hit Of The Morning Sun', 'Miss Lucifer', 'Autobahn 66', 'Detroit', 'Rise', 'The Lord Is My Shotgun', 'City', 'Some Velvet Morning', 'Skull X', 'A Scanner Darkly' and 'Space Blues#2'. And if there ever was a song called 'Bomb The Pentagon', then it was sensibly reworked and expunged from memory. Such a titled song was never officially recorded but of course they were accused of bottling it in fear of an American backlash. Without blatantly surrendering, Bobby attempted to present their case.

"The song was not all about dropping bombs on the pentagon," he said, "that was one line in the song. If you listen to the rest of the lyrics you can work out what the song's about. We only ever played it in that incarnation about four times. It was never, ever recorded. I ain't a bottler but I'm a songwriter and I can change any line that I want."

'Rise' appeared as the reworking of the controversially named song which, lyrically, seemed to be a straightforward narrative about Governments abusing trust and money. The offending phrase might have been appropriate in a different context but it regardless remains as confrontational as anything on the last album and, ironically, one of their finest songs of recent years. For Primal Scream the tiresome issue was considered closed, as they would sooner discuss the brand new songs, many of which as usual featured a number of friends offering their distinct services.

Jim Reid, who had been doing well since the demise of The Jesus And Mary Chain with his new band Freeheat, found time to provide lead vocals on 'Detroit', a snarling Kraftwerk-esque scurry through a bleak industrial wasteland of stomping beats and

revved-up guitars. 'The Lord Is My Shotgun' was decorated by the harmonica blowing of Robert Plant - the
former Led Zeppelin singer was drafted in to complete
a number that sounded not unlike Zeppelin's 'When
The Levee Breaks', yet with more of the contemporary
electro feel that Primal Scream always sought.

Kate Moss, the supermodel who had been friends
with the band since the early 90s, shared the vocals on
'Some Velvet Morning', an old Lee Hazlewood/Nancy
Sinatra number that was given a radical makeover.
"Kate's a good friend of mine," explained Bobby, "I
asked her if she'd do a duet on the album and she said
'I'd love to'. Her voice is really good, really European
and girlish but dead sexy." Singing lead vocals on
'Space Blues#2' was Martin Duffy, who displayed a
fragile and innocent sounding voice of which any
self-respecting choirboy would be proud.

Elsewhere, via David Holmes and more than two
years of tinkering, 'City' finally made it onto a Primal
Scream album and, with the word 'Sick' removed from
the title as a simple act of good faith, they were again
displaying their lurking affection for the likes of The
Stooges and MC5. Yet, like clockwork, their love of
stretching out and hammering those guitars
occasionally got the better of their equally successful
plans to make technology-driven music.

Then there was 'Deep Hit Of The Morning Sun', a processed sludge across a tribe of warped beats mixed with an archetypal Gillespie slur. Guitars sounded dark and tortured like the openers on the last two albums; introducing *Evil Heat* as another fiery statement, it paints a sleazy picture of post-apocalypse Britain. It was claustrophobic and intense, a mood counterbalanced by the homages 'Autobahn 66' and 'A Scanner Darkly'. The former, a worthy update of Kraftwerk's classic, was a melancholic waltz as good as anything since *Screamadelica* and the latter a glistening space age instrumental that whimsically attempted to soundtrack Philip K Dick's cult science fiction novel of the same name. The technology on both was controlled to their great advantage.

"A lot of musicians have techno fear," began one of Bobby's favourite speeches. "They're scared of being replaced. What they don't realise is that you can't replace inspiration. The sampler is an instrument as much as a guitar, the same as a drum machine's an instrument as much as a drum kit. It's there to be used, if you've got the imagination, you can use it properly to make great music." This proud attitude, perhaps, is the very reason why the anticipation of any new Primal Scream record is likened to the appeal of liquid mercury, or the equally elusive chameleon. They are a rock 'n' roll band, of that everyone's agreed, but still you just never knew what you were going to get.

Released by Sony via Columbia in August '02, *Evil Heat* only managed to enter the UK album chart at a disappointing number nine and didn't hang around the upper regions for very long either. First week sales were a mere sixteen thousand, down around fifty per cent from *Xtrmntr* two and a half years earlier. The critical response had been favourable, though hardly phenomenal.

Some of the more encouraging reviews included the *NME* boasting: "Even after most of our rock 'n' roll stars have disappeared up their own noses, Primal Scream remain class A contenders." *Q* wrote: "It's old stuff made thrillingly new and pretty much what this band do best." *Loaded* magazine: "Despite having a collective age of nearly two hundred, sickly child Bobby Gillespie and his pie-eyed friends still make a far more adventurous racket than any of their younger contemporaries. You've got to say hats off."

Most, though, couldn't help but mention the clouding Pentagon matter; suggesting that when their macho posturing of late was harshly brought into reality as mere entertainers, they definitely came off the worse.

Not that Primal Scream needed the press anymore, as unless something drastic happened to their maverick reputation, the record would sell the usual amount and keep everyone content until next time. But having worked as hard as ever on the album they of course wanted people to hear it. Thus the whirlwind publicity machine started up and it was alarmingly more friendly than ever.

The promotional campaign had begun with two sold out shows at the Shepherd's Bush Empire in June and had continued through several interviews, large outdoor festivals and TV shows. Alongside a sentimental appearance on *Top Of The Pops,* the band performed on *CD:UK,* hardly traditional Primal Scream territory. Yet a confident race through techno-stomper lead single 'Miss Lucifer' on the notorious teen show fitted neatly alongside the dancing kids one sleepy Saturday morning. Disguised by dark shades to distance themselves from the immaturity of it all, they launched into a less than perfect mime of the song but still looked to be enjoying themselves fully; jumping around the stage with the delight of a band half their age. In the make believe world of television, Andrew Innes made for a convincing drummer and Bobby, who was looking as skinny and as cool as ever, seemed more at home in front of the studio audience than he'd done before his own crowds for some time.

On the eve of the release of the album, the cable TV channel MTV2 screened a 'Primal Scream Weekend', during which they showed virtually all their videos in addition to edited highlights of a lengthy interview with Bobby and Mani. Some of the topics the pair discussed included recording the new album, the background behind some of their videos, live work and their collaborations with different producers. They appeared polite and easy going but it has to be said that for such a promised 'exclusive', they gave away little that couldn't have been predicted beforehand.

Without the swearing, they said much the same as they had for *Xtrmntr* but they looked cleaner, healthier and generally more interested in presenting themselves as likeable folks after all. Far from the sulking, mumbling disinterest that had once been a band trademark, their snappy, cheerful and funny answers provided a welcome relief.

That Primal Scream appeared more accessible was no doubt down to their relationship with a new record company. And that must have been strange. After all those years on Creation, where they were part of the family rather than just another roster-filling act, to be out there to please and make everyone aware of a new album could be regarded as the act of a band enjoying themselves, and Sony, taking no chances, provided them with a fully functional official internet website.

Like any other act in the twenty-first century, Primal Scream were benefiting massively from the world wide web. With dozens of fan sites already online, followers all over the world could interact, share news and opinions on everything from lyric interpretations to live reviews, the record company had little choice but to join the cyberspace revolution.

The internet was already the largest and fastest growing interactive medium and it seemed that having finally realised that it couldn't be efficiently policed, labels were having to offer all kinds temptations to help limit the demand for illegal recordings and unreliable gossip. The official site, like many, seemed light years behind the resourceful fan equivalents when it came to the latest news and overall appeared interested in presenting a languid style with slight and slow content. It did however make snatches of new material available before the album was released; the internet was at last being used in unity with record labels, perhaps facing up to a battle they seemed destined to lose. Meanwhile Primal Scream concentrated on a staggered series of live dates.

At the grand VIP re-opening of London's legendary Marquee club, they played what the few lucky fans who managed to get tickets described as the greatest show of their career. In the intimate confines of the new club they burned like alighting hipsters, unflappably strutting their rock star stuff, while the majority of the celebrity-littered audience forgot their cold reserve and howled for more soaring electro-riffing.

The fact that Primal Scream were considered totally in with London's glossy socialites was becoming ever-more apparent with the increasingly imaginative glam image of Bobby Gillespie who, deep down, knew very well that he loved the camera. He'd frequently been snapped hanging out with some of the world's top fashion designers and supermodels over the years, so it didn't come as a total surprise when he finally released his alter ego onto the catwalk before setting off for dates in Japan.

In a bizarre photo session for the *Transformer* series on Showstudio's leading fashion and design website, Bobby and girlfriend Katy modelled white suits, glitter scarves and slinky underwear courtesy of in vogue designers Alexander McQueen and Agent Provocateur. As the sequence progressed, the pair got ever more romantic, passing quite easily as another well-oiled model couple, equally capable of promoting an exotic perfume or deodorant. While Bobby wasn't the first rock star to give costume designers a little extra publicity, it was perhaps the ultimate example of how comfortable he'd become with the image. He'd no doubt laugh that it wasn't something to be taken seriously and it's hard to imagine him having done it in his twenties, or even as recently as *Xtrmntr*. He was a relaxed adult these days; the boys' club had matured and it appeared that the numbing hedonism of those days was well and truly over.

Sponsored by lager brand Carling, *Homecoming* was a series of music documentaries produced by London-based At It Productions for Channel Four. The premise of the series was to get a guided tour from the featured band around the places of their origin. Accompanied by an intimate concert, cut with views from close associates and clued-up music journalists, it was an attempt to destroy the myth, have them connect with their roots and provide some pretty interesting television. After steamrollering the UK throughout December before taking a break into 2003, it was the turn of Primal Scream to go under the microscope that had already presented the likes of The Manic Street Preachers and The Charlatans as loveable small town boys.

Word leaked via the Carling Live website that just five hundred places were being given away to see them perform for the programme. Applicants had to register with the site and correctly answer two simple questions about the band to be entered in the draw for tickets. Each winner was sent up to four guest passes just a week before the show.

The chosen venue was The Garage, a small first floor club towards the bottom of Sauchiehall Street in Glasgow's main shopping area; a location which used to house The Venue, where Primal Scream first performed officially nearly nineteen years earlier.

Doors were to open at seven and the band were due on at eight, a good three hours earlier than usual. Inside album artwork, Carling logos and classic Grant Fleming photographs were colourfully projected around the tiny L-shaped room, soon to be heaving with fresh-faced teens, indie veterans and young professionals, many of whom took full advantage of the sponsor's wares. People were politely giving vox pops to the omni-present camera crews and answering the oh-so-vital questions from Carling about just how much they drank. Primal Scream's performance was to the usual standard; including Kevin Shields, the seven of them were squashed together, leaving a greasy-haired Gillespie little room for his usual mic stand recklessness. He still managed to smash it to pieces though. They played a song by late New York Doll Johnny Thunders, appropriately titled for the famous addict, 'Born To Lose'.

After returning from America and a handful of club dates, an absolute best ever rip-it-up at Glastonbury preluded the broadcast which saw all the major players offering their views along, with David Holmes, Douglas Hart and journalists Roger Morton and John Robb. The fun but predictable forty minute programme was introduced by the voiceover of radio personality Jo Whiley. The filmmakers did their best to illustrate the band's origins by shooting what little remained of old Glasgow such as the tenement buildings, docklands and rundown housing estates, while interview snippets from the cast revealed some amusing home truths.

Robert claims to have hated Glasgow back then because if you were different you would be singled out, and that he'd had a guitar from about twelve or thirteen since his Gran won the pools and gave him a couple of hundred quid to fund escapism. Alan McGee recalled witnessing a hatchet attack at school and Bobby remembers that despite being three years his senior he initially knew Robert because he'd lived in the next street to him. A surprisingly talkative Mr

Young also let slip that Bobby used to hang speakers out his window and play everybody in the neighbourhood his newly-purchased punk singles.

In with all the nostalgic quips however Gillespie momentarily let his guard slip. His one revealing comment was of course immediately retracted. Amid the ego polishing he said: "I think the band's got better because we weeded out the weak musicians," as if to finally explain why there had been so many temporary members over the years, but no sooner had his words split the air than he backpedalled: "no, that sounds too cruel, no disrespect to anybody that played with us before but finally we're truly happy."

It was the same chink that had characterised him for years. The programme was an entertaining if somewhat slight overview of the band's history, that ended with Robert saying with a giggle that they may well be remembered as "a bunch of hedonistic nutcases that could have achieved a lot more but didn't quite get it."

long life

For a band who'd built up a list of members in the past nineteen years that read like the population of a small country, the current harmony between Bobby Gillespie, Andrew Innes, Robert Young, Martin Duffy and Gary Mounfield is the most reassuring sign yet that whether it be with age, parenthood, the parole of Satpal Ram or just a plain love of what they do, Primal Scream seem totally sure of themselves and know exactly where their strengths lie. Of late none of the core members have left, there have been no shaky live shows, postponements, fall-outs with management, near deaths or anything like the tumultuous events that have chequered their past. It has taken a while but they have found themselves.

"It's the best band we've ever had," declared Bobby, though certainly not for the first time. But now though, with this current line-up, he could resolutely claim they'd produced three consistently excellent albums in a row, and while *Evil Heat* was probably not the very best effort of their career, it was only because, post-*Screamadelica*, listeners' standards were so impossibly high.

For better or worse, that timeless 1991 album will likely always stand as their crowning glory, an album that absolutely everyone adores, that like all the best music instantly reminds listeners of where they were when songs like 'Loaded', 'Come Together' and 'Higher Than The Sun' leaked everywhere from the speakers of nightclubs, to chart radio stations to dope fuelled student house parties. The bright, drug-themed kaleidoscope collection that saved their record company from going bankrupt may very well, even now, be lurking around the lower regions of the British album charts, as it remains, as one leading magazine put it: "The E generation's Sgt Pepper."

Having flown too close to the sun with *Screamadelica*, their retreat was the contrived *Give Out But Don't Give Up*, a record they apparently can't bear to listen to nowadays. While that may sound harsh, especially considering their great affection for trad rock, that whole belief now appears over-thought, clunky and genuinely uncomfortable with them - they have always preferred to wipe the slate clean with each new release. But it shouldn't be forgotten that *Give Out...* is still the sound of a band in love with what they do and the next time someone dusts it off and gives it a spin, they'll be be surprised at just how fun it can be. It was an album and an image, that simply came and went.

If they had never recorded another note after those two records, Primal Scream would always be remembered for producing two of the most fascinating and contrary statements of the 90s. While the former was incandescent with freshness and adored emotion, the latter was justly the product of a young, newly wealthy band living out their fantasies with a rich and varied journey into the heartland of their musical heritage. And there can be no doubt that they had a great time doing so which, after all, is largely the whole point of being in a rock 'n' roll band.. remember?

Since then, with the line-up settled, the records have been more focused and consistent. They've become more intense and reflective of the dark world they see but that's not to say that Primal Scream are obsessive moaners who see little good in humankind, it's just been a theme like any other in their sprawling career. It's been an exciting ride following them thus far, and while there have inevitably been some disappointments along the way, they stand as only more evidence of them doing whatever they felt like at that moment, be it an uncertain or assured success. And considering the size of some of those risks with all the different styles of music, the fact that the hits finally outnumber the misses is credit to their uncannily accurate foresights and loyal fans staying with them throughout.

Noticeably, audiences at shows appear to have aged with them yet, unlike many fans who stay faithful to a touring act, new material always seems to be as appreciated as the greatest hits; their back catalogue looks just that, something to be proud of but not dwell on. In addition fans don't come across as hooligans or hit single tourists but intelligent people who understand their need to move on while trying their utmost to entertain.

"Every time something goes wrong on stage, we're all laughing," said Bobby, "so we aren't pompous, serious musicians, we're punk rockers. I want people to get off on our music, I want it to be affirmative and even the more abstract, fractured stuff I think people can relate to because they feel like that." A typically defensive yet reassuring comment.

Whereas Mani has taken some of the workload off Bobby by handling the interviews of late, the singer still remains largely the lone face of the band. He'd quickly assert that he does nothing but give his opinion when asked for it and, to his credit, despite the occasional ambiguity to which we're all prone, he certainly isn't the hypocrite the music press would have you believe. Bobby says what he thinks about what he knows, never ignorant of music of different genres or eras and if anything he is just too proud of music he cares passionately about. But, notably, what he very rarely talks about these days is his relationship with his bandmates when not on duty.

Internally, if say they weren't as close as they had been, or the band was no longer the most important thing in their lives, then fans would simply never find out. Bobby and Mani can boast all day about how their togetherness is stronger than ever but because they do it could easily be taken for granted. They are comfortable with how they present themselves and more than once devoted fans and the like have learned the hard way that they are actually a very private group indeed. They let out only what they want and don't appear to hesitate on occasion to slam closed the access doors.

By the end of 2002, Bobby was far more likely to appear on the cover of the chic lifestyle monthlies aimed at Britain's young urban professionals than the *NME*, the paper that was so helpful to his band in the late 80s and early 90s. Nowadays the *Express* doesn't sell nearly as many as it did during Primal Scream's climb to reverence, as audiences, both listeners and readers have fragmented in the eras since, moving on with technology that is faster and more efficient than the established press could ever be. The band know full well that things don't stay the same, especially not in the entertainment industries, but to the fans, lest we forget, the music will always linger.

Thirteen years after 'Loaded' had everyone trying to wire their jaws back together following the astonishment of its startling fusion of rock and dance, and nearly twenty since Bobby's 'just whack them' interpretation of how to drum with The Jesus And Mary Chain, Primal Scream are still doing their thing in a rapid here-today-gone-tomorrow music culture. From the jangly pop of their earliest days, through hard rock, dance, dub, punk and gospel and other genres inbetween, they've gained a colossal reputation as innovators, leading the way for new fads before moving on, blending styles with their own often inspired musical vision. Their influence on British post-punk music can be found on numerous bands from the same and later generations, but they can even more fruitfully claim to have helped develop the groundbreaking careers of artists like The Jesus And Mary Chain, Andy Weatherall, The Chemical Brothers and Asian Dub Foundation to name but a few.

Their home, Creation Records was, for a while there in the mid to late 90s, pretty much the most publicised record company on earth, as it took until Oasis for people to realise that along with Alan McGee, their enthusiasm and passion for music had helped build a story that was as inspirational as that of any British independent. The label was 'all about allowing crazies to make crazy music' and Primal Scream have undoubtedly made some crazy music that just wouldn't have seen the light of day elsewhere. Those who deserve the praise already know who they are.

While all this may rightly indicate that it's a very good time to look back on the amazing career of Primal Scream, such retrospectives do not sit comfortably with Bobby Gillespie. Their mentioned first book, written by long-time friend and touring DJ Kris Needs, apparently isn't a tell-all biography but rather a poring discussion about their favourite music. It's evidently far too early for nostalgia, something that Bobby confirmed when stating in 2002 that his one wish for the future was just that "the band stayed together and kept making great music."

discography

SONIC FLOWER GROOVE (SEPTEMBER '87)

LP UK ELEVATION ELV 2
CD EUROPE WARNER 242182-2 (RE-RELEASE '91)
CD JP WARNER (WPCR-64)*
CD JP WARNER (WPCR-1328)
3:45 Gentle Tuesday
3:12 Treasure Trip
2:40 May The Sun Shine Bright For You
2:34 Sonic Sister Love
3:47 Silent Spring
3:36 Imperial
4:43 Love You
3:30 Leaves
2:44 Aftermath
3:22 We Go Down Slowly Rising
Produced by Mayo Thompson
All songs written by Beattie, Gillespie
* Contains hidden bonus tracks; 'Black Star Carnival', 'I'm Gonna Make You Mine', 'Star Fruit Rider', 'So Sad About Us', 'Imperial' (demo) from the Gentle Tuesday and Imperial singles.*
Japanese CD contains unofficial lyrics.

PRIMAL SCREAM (SEPTEMBER '89)

LP UK CREATION CRELP 054*

CD UK Creation CRECD 054
CD JP Epic/Sony ESCA 5946
CD JP Epic/Sony ESCA-7701 ['98 reissue]
3:02 Ivy Ivy Ivy
4:38 You're Just Dead Skin To Me
3:05 She Power
3:06 You're Just Too Dark To Care
5:07 I'm Losing More Than I'll Ever Have
2:28 Gimme Gimme Teenage Head
3:06 Lone Star Girl
3:28 Kill The King
2:16 Sweet Pretty Thing
1:43 Jesus Can't Save Me
Produced by Sister Anne (Primal Scream)
* Contains Free Ltd 7" with demos with initial copies of LP
Split Wide Open (Demo)
Lone Star Girl (Demo)
All songs written by Gillespie, Innes, Young.
Japanese CD contains unofficial lyrics.

SCREAMADELICA (SEPTEMBER '91)

LP UK Creation CRELP 076
CD UK Creation CRECD 076
CD UK Creation CRECD 076P [Promo]
MD UK Creation CREMD 076
CD US Sire 2-26714°°
CD JP Epic/Sony (ESCA 5946)
LP UK (reissued in 2001 on 180g vinyl)
3:47 Movin' On Up*°
5:14 Slip Inside This House**
6:50 Don't Fight It Feel It (featuring Denise Johnson)
3:35 Higher Than The Sun*
4:58 Inner Flight
10:17 Come Together (Andy Weatherall-Extended)*
7:00 Loaded (Extended)

5:35 Damaged*°
5:57 I'm Coming Down
7:34 Higher Than The Sun - A Dub Symphony In Two Parts (featuring Jah Wobble).
3:43 Shine Like Stars
Produced by Andrew Weatherall and assisted by Hugo Nicholson for Boys Own Productions.
* Produced by the Orb (Dr. Alex Patterson and Thrash)
° Produced by Andrew Weatherall.
** Produced by Hypnotone and Andrew Innes. Additional Production Andrew Weatherall.
*° Mixed by Jimmy Miller. Additional Production by Jimmy Miller.
The US CD has Terry Farley mix instead of Andy Weatherall Mix of 'Come Together' which has vocals. This version also appeared on the UK single.
°° There was also a limited edition US Promo Picture CD with sun logo with same catalogue no. as the US version CD.
All songs written by Gillespie, Innes, Young. Except 'Slip Inside This House' by Hall / Erickson
Japanese CD contains unofficial lyrics.

GIVE OUT BUT DON'T GIVE UP (MARCH '94)

CD UK CREATION CRECD146
CD US SIRE/CREATION
CD JP EPIC/SONY ESCA 5944
MD JP EPIC/SONY ESCA 1044
LP UK CREATION CRELP146°
3:44 Jailbird
3:34 Rocks
4:27 (I'm Gonna) Cry Myself Blind
5:23 Funky Jam
4:11 Big Jet Plane
5:20 Free

3:49 Call on Me
8:27 Struttin'
3:24 Sad And Blue
6:14 Give Out But Don't Give Up
6:26 I'll Be There For You
5:22 Everybody Needs Somebody*
Hidden Bonus Track
° *Came with a print of Cover.*
All songs written by Gillespie, Innes, Young. Except 'Give Out..' by Gillespie, Innes, Young and Clinton

There was an Australian promo pre-release cassette with some of the tracks with slightly different names.

There was a Japanese promo only press kit folder that contained a book, a copy of the CD, and the promo only Japan compilation CD called 'Souls'

Japanese CD contains unofficial lyrics

VANISHING POINT (JULY '97)

CD UK CREATION CRECD178
CD US REPRISE 2-46559-AB [PROMO]
CD JP EPIC/SONY (ESCA 6688)*
LP UK CREATION CRELP178
MC UK CREATION CCREMC178
MD ECC
7:06 Burning Wheel
4:09 Get Duffy
5:48 Kowalski
4:24 Star
3:01 If They Move, Kill 'Em
3:59 Out Of The Void
5:36 Stuka
3:52 Medication

3:27 Motorhead
8:04 Trainspotting °
3:50 Longlife
Produced by Brendan Lynch and Primal Scream.
° Produced by Andrew Weatherall.
All songs written by Gillespie, Innes, Young, Duffy except 'Kowalski' by Gillespie, Innes, Young, Duffy and Mounfield and 'Motorhead' by Kilmister.
* Contains 'Jesus' as a bonus track.
Japanese CD contains unofficial lyrics as well.

EchoDek (October '97)

CD UK Creation CRECD 224*
CD JP Epic/Sony ESCA 6844
LP UK Creation CRELP 224P
7x5 UK Creation CRE 224°
Living Dub (Long Life)
Duffed Up (Get Duffy)
Revolutionary (Star)
JU-87 (Stuka)
First Name unknown (Kowalski)
Vanishing Dub Vain in Dub (Out of the Void)
Last Train (Trainspotting)
Wise Blood (Stuka)
Dub in Vain (Medication)
Produced by Brendan Lynch and Primal Scream.
Remixed by Adrian Sherwood.
All songs written by Gillespie, Innes, Young, Duffy except 'Kowalski' by Gillespie, Innes, Young, Duffy and Mounfield.
* Special limited edition version comes in special brown cardboard package that has a magnet that seals it. A jewel

box version also exists. Both have the same catalogue no.

° *Ltd 5x7" Box set. Comes with booklet and 45 adapter -* *(4500 copies). This looks almost exactly like the ltd CD but in a 1"x 5"x 5" box.*

Promo pre-release 12" vinyl version exists but it does not contain 'Dub in Vain'.

XTRMNTR (EXTERMINATOR) (JANUARY '00)

CD UK CREATION CRECD239
CD UK CREATION CRECD239P [PROMO ONLY]*
CD US ASTRALWERKS 49260 (MAY 2, 2000)
LP UK CREATION CRELP239°
MD UK CREATION CREMD239
MC UK CREATION CCRE239
CD JP EPIC/SONY ESCA 8106 (19 JANUARY 2000)*
4:57 Kill All Hippies
3:41 Accelerator
5:50 Exterminator
7:04 Swastika Eyes (Jagz Kooner's Spectre mix)
4:16 Pills
7:01 Blood Money
5:23 Keep Your Dreams
3:33 Insect Royalty
6:44 MBV Arkestra
6:33 Swastika Eyes (Chemical Brothers mix)
5:19 Shoot Speed Kill Light

All Songs Written By Primal Scream (EMI / Copyright Control / Complete Music) Except Track 1 By Primal Scream / M.Nelson / Discovery Productions Inc (Emi / Copyright Control / Complete Music / Copyright Control / Discovery Productions Inc) & Track 10 By Rusty Evans / Victoria Pike (Copyright Control).

EVIL HEAT (AUG '02)

CD UK Columbia/Sony
CD JP Sony ESCA-8169 or SICP144 (30 July 2002)
CD Aus Sony 5088512000 (5 Aug 2002)
3:45 Deep Hit Of Morning Sun
3:02 Miss Lucifer
6:15 Autobahn 66
3:03 Detroit
4:21 Rise
4:05 The Lord Is My Shotgun
3:28 City
3:52 Some Velvet Morning
3:52 Skull X
4:30 A Scanner Darkly
2.32 Space Blues #2

This discography was compiled by Hans Gylling and Jeff Birgbauer. My thanks for letting us use it.

Index